PRIMATOLOGISTS' TES

CW00420710

"One of the world's foremost primat(
his life as an American who embraced his Scottish ancestry and
sought adventures in Africa to follow chimpanzees through their
natural habitat. Funny, warm, unexpected, and with attention
to behavioral details of both humans and apes."

Frans de Waal, author of *Mama's Last Hug: Animal Emotions
and What They Tell Us about Ourselves*

"In case you have never tried it, chasing after chimpanzees can
be hilarious. So is Bill McGrew's book of that title chronicling
how a young man from Oklahoma came to be awarded a Rhodes
Scholarship and after Oxford found himself plunked down in
charge of a colony of chimpanzees in Louisiana with a penchant
for jail-breaking. Later he would travel to Africa and over a long
career study wild chimpanzees at nine different sites - a primatological record. It is how McGrew came to be the world's expert
on the richness and diversity of chimpanzee cultures as well as
a wry commentator on the comedic aspects of the lives of those
who study them."

Sarah Blaffer Hrdy, author of *Mothers and Others: The Evolutionary Origins of Mutual Understanding*

"Follow Bill McGrew on his life's journey, or how a young
naturalist and athlete from Oklahoma through luck and pluck
ended up studying wild chimpanzees and founding cultural
primatology."

Carel van Schaik, author of *Among Orangutans: Red Apes and
the Rise of Human Culture*

"Renowned primatologist Bill McGrew has written a lovely memoir, constructed as a series of vignettes about key moments in his life and career. *Chasing after Chimpanzees* is a heartfelt glimpse into one scientist's fascinating life and a thoroughly enjoyable read."

Craig Stanford, author of *The New Chimpanzee*

"Bill McGrew has invited you on the adventure of a lifetime. This memoir is essential reading for any aspiring scientist and for those of us more advanced in our years. Each vignette holds advice and inspiration as prolific as his career."

Crickette Sanz, author of *Tool Use in Animals: Cognition and Ecology*

"I first met Bill McGrew at a primatology conference 30+ years ago, when he kindly chatted with me - a rank novice - about a talk I gave and have enjoyed crossing paths ever since. I very much enjoyed reading his memoir, given his exceptionally rich and unusual life."

Anne Russon, author of *The Evolution of Thought: Evolution of Great Ape Intelligence*

Chasing after Chimpanzees

The Making of a Primatologist

William C McGrew

Emeritus Professor of Evolutionary Primatology,
University of Cambridge

Honorary Professor, School of Psychology & Neuroscience,
University of St Andrews

Mereo Books

2nd Floor, 6-8 Dyer Street, Cirencester, Gloucestershire, GL7 2PF
An imprint of Memoirs Books. www.mereobooks.com
and www.memoirsbooks.co.uk

CHASING AFTER CHIMPANZEES
ISBN: 978-1-86151-582-7

First published in Great Britain in 2021
by Mereo Books, an imprint of Memoirs Books.

The address for Memoirs Books can be
found at www.mereobooks.com

Mereo Books Ltd. Reg. No. 12157152

Typeset in 11/18pt Sabon
by Wiltshire Associates.
Printed and bound in Great Britain

To *Pan troglodytes*
for everything

.

CONTENTS

Preface

Chronology

EARLY DAYS

ADULTHOOD

ACADEMIA

FIELDWORK

PREFACE

After more than three-quarters of a century, it seems time to contemplate, to try to account for a career now mostly spent. But why does a person turn to autobiography? It could be to provide a coherent and considered story to pass on to one's descendants, but I have no known biological offspring, therefore no children, grandchildren, etc. However, I do have academic offspring, in the form of former students, especially those who gained PhDs and so begat more students. Or it could be to inform kin, friends and colleagues, who know bits and pieces but not the whole of a person's life story. It could be to give the world informative, maybe even useful, knowledge based on lessons learned in a lifetime of scholarship, but I'm no intellectual luminary, just a naturalist who chased chimpanzees for decades. It could be self-indulgence, making use of idle time in retirement (or Covid lockdown!) to take strolls down 'memory lane', revisiting times past, retrieving them to savour, while time and memory still allow. Or it simply could be narcissism. Or all of the above?

What form should such an exercise take? It could be a chronological prose narrative, told chapter by chapter from birth to present, but such an account can make dry and dull reading. Instead, I have chosen a different format, based on notable events (highlights?) of a long life: vignettes recounting what are to me notable experiences that might be engaging, perhaps revealing, even amusing. (Of course, only the reader can say if this is the case!) These life-snippets are in four sections, but they emphasise a life invested in primatology, grounded in Africa and based on years spent on that continent. They range in length but most are short, averaging about 500 words. These stories need a skeleton on which to hang, a framework to provide sequence and continuity, so a bare-bones chronology is provided at the outset.

I was the first of four children born to William and Dorothy McGrew. My father led a double life as a university professor and in private practice as a certified public accountant. My mother was a homemaker, with a hard-won but unused degree in zoology. Growing up in Norman, Oklahoma, in the 1950s was quiet and mainstream. I attended only one school from nursery school through high school, then went on to study at the University of Oklahoma. Thus my upbringing was hometown-bound, until I graduated in 1965. At 21 years of age, I left Oklahoma and never lived there again.

I moved to the United Kingdom, and, except for one substantial interlude (1993-2005 in Oxford, Ohio), I have lived on the east side of the Atlantic ever since. As a 'faculty brat', I had been unknowingly set for a career in higher education. The career path was orthodox: doctoral studies (Oxford), post-doctoral research (Edinburgh, Stanford), and eventually a first permanent faculty position (Stirling). Decades later, I finished up at Cambridge, as Professor of Evolutionary Primatology, but along the way, I had brief stints at North Carolina-Charlotte, New Mexico, Earlham, and California-Berkeley. In retirement in rural Fife, I dawdle along as an Honorary Professor in Psychology and Neuroscience at the University of St Andrews.

What (if anything) perhaps makes my life worth noting was time spent with chimpanzees, mostly wild ones, over 40 years (1972-2012) and what that taught me. I was lucky enough to be paid by various academic institutions to do what I would have paid them to let me do. Hence those apes have key prominence in this effort, from title onwards. The scientific results of these labours are in books and journal articles, to be found easily by googling, but here I recount events that are mean to add flesh to the scholarly skeleton.

Inevitably, there are some caveats, some self-imposed constraints to this academic memoir: the vignettes say little about my private life and almost nothing about spouses or lovers. More is said about colleagues than friends, but little is said about enemies. Also absent is the usual list of fulsome acknowledgements to those who helped me along the way, although such lists are in my single-authored books. Instead, I note students and early-career researchers, for whom I have been somewhat responsible, officially or otherwise, and to whom I am grateful for their company on my academic journey. To those who recognise themselves or others who don't, I apologise if these inclusions cause any offence. I do here acknowledge my thanks to those who helped bring this book to fruition: Jim Anderson, Evelyn Boxall, Adrian Hernandez-Aguilar, Jackie MacPherson, Larry McGrew, Alejandra Pascual-Garrido, Tim Londergan, Wulf Schiefenhoevel, Miranda Stocks, Elizabeth Williamson, and especially Agumi Inaba. Special thanks to Chris Newton and Toni Tingle for their help and patience in making this book happen.

Sceptical readers may wonder at the relevance of some of the early reminiscences, especially in the first two sections, for chimpanzees or primatology. Some (Early Gender Bending) are referred to later. Others' relevance is straightforwardly implied, such as the importance of physical fitness and stamina for field work (26.2 Miles, West Highland Way). Others have less obvious implications: Skiing the Iron Curtain is less about skiing and more about acquiring skills in unofficial currency exchange. Super Bowl Surprise is less about football and more about coping with armed offenders. Others may be indicative or suggestive of important general experiences or attitudes (Coaching, Never Again!). Finally, some admittedly have no obvious relevance (at least discernible to me) but could be informative to readers. I beg their indulgence!

About the format: As the vignettes are numbered, they can be cross-referenced to others on the same or related topics. I apologise for some redundancy across vignettes, but it is sometimes needed to help each one stand on its own. At the end of some vignettes are references for keen readers who may wish to pursue the topics into the scientific literature. Scientific names of species are omitted, to make the text less stodgy.

All proceeds from this book will go to organisations that rescue and care for chimpanzees: Liberia Chimpanzee Rescue and Protection, Monrovia, Liberia (www.liberiachimpanzeerescue.org); Lwiro Primates, Democratic Republic of Congo (www.lwiroprimates.org); MONA, Girona, Spain (www.fundacionmona.org); Takaguma Chimpanzee Sanctuary, Freetown, Sierra Leone (www.tacugama.com).

Finally, to allay any doubts: I chased *after* chimpanzees, not to catch them but to try to stay up with them in order to observe their daily lives. Happily for me, enough of them did so!

Cupar, Fife, Scotland, 4 Sept. 2021

CHRONOLOGY

1944 Born in Fort Smith, Arkansas, USA

1962 Graduated University High School, Norman, Oklahoma, USA

1962-65 Undergraduate studies, University of Oklahoma, Norman. BSc in Zoology (minors in History and Mathematics)

1965-70 Postgraduate studies, Rhodes Scholar, University of Oxford, England, Dept. of Zoology ('65-66), Inst. of Experimental Psychology ('66-68)

1970 DPhil in Psychology, University of Oxford. Thesis: *An Ethological Study of Social Behaviour in Preschool Children*

1968 Population Council Fellow, Dept. of Psychology, University of Edinburgh, Scotland

1969 National Institutes of Mental Health Fellow, Dept. of Psychology, Univ. of Edinburgh

1970-71 Social Science Research Council Postdoctoral Research Associate, Dept. of Psychology, University of Edinburgh

1972 Visiting Investigator, Delta Regional Primate Research Center, Covington, Louisiana, USA

1972-73 Research Associate, Dept. of Psychiatry and Behavioral Sciences, Stanford University, and Gombe Stream Research Centre, Kigoma, Tanzania

1974-81 Lecturer in Psychology, University of Stirling, Scotland

1976-79 Stirling African Primate Project, Mt. Assirik, Niokolo-Koba National Park, Senegal

1980 Visiting Faculty Member, Dept. of Psychology, Univ. of North Carolina - Charlotte, USA

1981-89 Senior Lecturer in Psychology, University of Stirling

1982 Nuffield Foundation Social Science Research Fellow, University of Stirling

1986 Visiting Faculty Member, Depts. of Anthropology and Biology, University of New Mexico, Albuquerque, USA

1989-92 Reader in Psychology, University of Stirling

1990 PhD in Social Anthropology, University of Stirling

Thesis: *Chimpanzee Material Culture: Implications for Human Evolution*

1993 Visiting Faculty Member, Dept. of Biology, Earlham College, Richmond, Indiana, USA

1993 Wiepking Distinguished Professor, Depts. of Sociology & Anthropology, Psychology and Zoology, Miami University, Oxford, Ohio, USA

1994 Visiting Professor, Dept. of Anthropology, University of California, Berkeley, USA

1994-2005 Professor, Depts. of Anthropology and Zoology, Miami University

1995 Outstanding Research Award, Center for Research into Anthropological Foundations of Technology, Indiana University, Bloomington, USA

1996 W.W. Howells Book Prize in Biological Anthropology, American Anthropological Association

1998 Prix Delwart, for Human Ethology and Cultural Anthropology, Fondation Jean-Marie Delwart & Royal Academy of Sciences of Belgium, Bruxelles

2001 Visiting Professor, Ecole des Hautes Etudes en Sciences Sociales, College de France, Paris

2001 Russell Trust Senior Research Fellow, School of Psychology, University of St. Andrews, Scotland

2003 Bye-Fellow, Selwyn College, and Visiting Research Fellow, Leverhulme Centre for Human Evolutionary Studies, University of Cambridge, England

2003 Fellow, Collegium Budapest, Hungary

2003 Elected Corresponding Fellow, Royal Society of Edinburgh, Scotland

2005 Elected Fellow, American Association for the Advancement of Science, USA

2008 Osman Hill Medal, Primate Society of Great Britain

2008-16 Fellow, Corpus Christi College, Cambridge

2009 PhD (by incorporation) in Biological Anthropology, University of Cambridge

2009-11 Professor of Evolutionary Primatology, University of Cambridge

2010 Visiting Fellow, Hanse-Wissenschaftskolleg, Delmenhorst, Germany

2010 Distinguished Alumni Award, College of Arts and Sciences, University of Oklahoma

2011 Emeritus Professor, University of Cambridge

2012 Senior Fellow, McDonald Institute for Archaeological Research, University of Cambridge

2016- Honorary Professor, School of Psychology and Neuroscience, University of St Andrews

2017 Retired to Fife, Scotland

EARLY DAYS

1 BIG WIND

Oklahoma is spared most extreme natural forces, such as earthquake, hurricane, landslide, tsunami, typhoon, volcano, etc, but it does have tornadoes...

When my father returned from WWII, he joined many others in going back to college, in his case, the University of Oklahoma. Universities were deluged by large numbers of veterans, and accommodation was short, especially for families. I was only four years old then, and my younger brother Larry, was only one. The four of us ended up in disused, all-wooden military barracks, abandoned at the war's end and acquired by the university for housing students.

One afternoon, my mother drove into town for grocery shopping, leaving us brothers at home with our father. Later, the tornado warning sirens began to sound. We knew what they were, because of test drills, but this one did not end soon; instead it went on and on. It took only a glance out the window for my father to spring into action. There was no time to head to the tornado shelter. He had us lie on the floor, threw a double bed mattress on top of us, and lay down on top of it.

Then there was a sound as if a giant railroad locomotive was speeding right through our apartment. Even muffled under the mattress, we heard an overwhelmingly loud noise, new to us. As quickly as it came, it went, and my father lifted up the mattress to set us free. We noticed lots of broken glass on the floor, as all the windows had been blown out, and the window screens and doors were torn off too. When we went outside, we saw shards of glass driven into the wooden side of the building, liked stabbed knives. Woe to anyone who'd been outside or even standing up indoors! They'd have been cut to ribbons.

But what of my mother? She'd been on her way home, in the car, when she saw the black clouds and the twister in the distance. She pulled the car over to the side of the road and lay down in a ditch. Luckily, the tornado passed by elsewhere. (Tornado damage can be almost unbelievably focused, unlike other types of wind-storms. A twister can level houses on one side of a street while leaving houses on the other side untouched.) Others were not so lucky as she, and people were killed in the building next to us.

Fast forward a few decades and now the US Government research facility for research on severe weather is sited at that same location. Oklahoma is in 'Tornado Alley', which runs north-south down the Great Plains. Nowadays, 'storm chasers' in vehicles record stunning photos and videos of tornadoes in action.

You might think that I would be traumatised by such an experience, but my clearest memory is of the Red Cross coming round to supply food, drink and blankets. Best of all, they had an apparently unlimited supply of doughnuts to distribute, and we could have as many as we wanted!

2 EARLY GENDER-BENDING

As a youth, I attended University School, run by the Dept. of Education of the University of Oklahoma. It was my educational base from nursery school to high school graduation

(1948-1962). We were a state school but of an unusual type, being, among other things, experimental subjects for various progressive initiatives in education. One of these experiences occurred in junior high school, when my class was 13 years old. Until that point, all school subjects were co-educationally taught, except for physical education and practical skills. In the latter, the boys did 'shop' (mostly carpentry) and the girls did home economics (mostly cooking).

Then, for reasons opaque to us boys in seventh grade, the girls asked why they were not allowed to work wood too. They wanted to make birdhouses, etc., like the boys. Apparently, no one could think of a really good reason *not* to allow this, so it happened.

But what about the reverse? We gender-bound lads were sceptical, to say the least, about home economics, but the teacher cleverly told us that our first class project would be to learn how to make our own pizzas! This was irresistible to budding adolescents with big appetites. Then, once we got used to wearing aprons, she led us over the semester through other simple cooking skills. Both genders got their crossover experiences. Sauce for the goose was also sauce for the gander, and vice versa! Later at Assirik, *all* members of the team did *all* chores, in rotation (see **90, 94**).

3 INTRODUCTION TO CHIMPANZEES

Intellectually or academically, I didn't meet chimpanzees until well into my post-doctoral career, having spent most of my postgraduate time doing ethological studies of pre-school-aged children. Many years before, my father had provided an introduction to the apes, without intending to do so, thus unwittingly setting the stage for my career. Besides being a university professor of accounting, he also practised income tax accounting, as a certified public accountant. His clients were often university colleagues, one being Prof. William Lemmon, a clinical psychologist. Lemmon was a larger-than-life character in several ways, especially in the 1950s: shaved head, alpha male attitude, orchid fancier, and parrot breeder. His avocation was Psych Services Inc., as head of a consortium of clinical psychologists providing private therapeutic treatment. Some of these colleagues collaborated with him by rearing chimpanzees in their homes, got from a breeding colony of these apes who lived on Lemmon's farm. The most famous of these was Lucy, raised by Maurice and Jane Temerlin, who later sought our advice about Lucy's emigrating to Africa (but that is another story).

Lemmon also had students, one of whom, Sue Savage-Rumbaugh, went on to a prestigious if unusual career of teaching human sign language to apes. (She was the first primatologist to publish in a scientific journal with apes as co-authors.) Another, Wayne McGuire, was later convicted (wrongly) of the murder of Dian Fossey, of *Gorillas in the Mist* fame (see **49**). Other University of Oklahoma students of primatology were Janis Carter, Barbara King and Janette Wallis. A one-time resident at Lemmon's farm was Washoe, the most famous sign-language-using chimpanzee of all, who worked lifelong with Roger and Debbie Fouts. Nim Chimpsky, the sign-language-trained chimpanzee whose reputed lack of accomplishments led to the downfall of 'pongo-linguistics', was also a one-time resident. It was an eventful place!

So, as a child, when I tagged along with my father picking up or dropping off tax papers, I became acquainted with a species of primate that would later determine my life for four decades. However, what I heard and saw at Lemmon's farm had little in common with what I later learned from their wild counterparts.

4 FISHING AND HUNTING

Growing up in Oklahoma, at least for boys, meant learning to fish. (This may surprise those who think of the state as arid grassland in the southern Great Plains, but Oklahoma has many impounded rivers yielding large lakes. Just don't look for salmon!) I caught my first fish, a catfish, at age 11 years, on a Boy Scout camp-out. It went home with me for my mother to cook, after my father and I prepared it.

The real source of fishing apprenticeship came from my uncle, 'Thrash' (Albert) Thrasher. He was a taciturn man, addicted to the sport, who preferred to practise it at night, usually in patient silence. I spent those evenings in contemplation, waiting for the bobber to start bouncing on the water's surface, signalling that a crappie or bluegill was biting. From the mentoring, I gained the confidence to take my bamboo pole and jar of grasshoppers or earthworms to fish at the local public golf course ponds. Again, my mother patiently cooked the small sunfish that sometimes resulted from these expeditions. Use of the word 'patience' twice in the preceding paragraph reflects its paramount virtue in fishing.

Later, my father, my brother Larry and I fished in various ways on several Oklahoma lakes. Sometimes we trolled lures behind a slow-moving open boat, seeking white bass. Sometimes we anchored offshore, preferably near a 'baited hole', composed of sunken tree limbs, said to attract fish (but more often seeming to tangle our lines), using minnows for bait. Sometimes we used spinning reels to cast special lures ('plugs') meant to tempt large-mouthed bass, which were big enough to put up a real fight. Sometimes we fished from bridges, high above the water, which meant that a hooked fish often flipped free before one could get it in hand. Finally, in colder weather, we resorted to fishing in special floating fishing barges, complete with heating, picnic chairs, and even soft drink and snack machines. Perhaps the apex of our family fishing came with catching cutthroat trout in Lake Yellowstone.

In adulthood, I rarely fish (see **91**). I once tried fly-fishing for trout on the River Tweed in the Scottish Borders, with my friend, Brian Fay, but it is clearly an acquired skill, to be tackled only by those with dedication. That day we caught only one fish, a tiddler, which we took home and fed to the cat. In Lake Tanganyika, I enjoyed fishing for various exotic but always tasty fish, including the fearsome Nile perch. The best fishing for me was at Assirik, in barely more than a stream reduced to isolated pools in the dry season, which usually meant catching the hardy, drought-resistant catfish. These days, I sometimes fish with my brother from his party-boat on Lake Ouachita, Arkansas, well-stocked with cold beer and comfy cushions, or from its dock, if we are lazy.

On the other hand, I have never hunted, nor felt the need to do so. I've never owned or fired a shotgun, so pheasants and ducks were safe from me, though I admit to having eaten them with relish (actually, with cranberry sauce). In fact, I've only once fired a rifle as part of obligatory target shooting while in the Reserve Officers' Training Corps (ROTC) (see **9, 39**). (ROTC classes were required for all able-bodied males during the first two years of higher education at state universities, such as the University of Oklahoma). We learned useful skills, such as compass navigation, which was later essential in field research, and how to spit-shine our shoes.

Why did I lack motivation to hunt? In Boy Scouts, our troop was taken for a tour of a meat-packing plant (abattoir) in Oklahoma City. We saw, close up, the whole process, from noisy cattle and pigs being herded up ramps to be killed, to the silent end-products, neatly-butchered chops and steaks headed for the supermarkets. The experience was graphic and gruesome enough for some of the boys to be sick and excused from continuing the tour. Decades later, I stopped eating mammals, perhaps a long-delayed effect to this subconsciously buried exposure to the animals' fate?

5 PRECOCIAL OPPORTUNITIES

In 1958, at age 14 years, I spent my first summer away from home and family, working as a 'kitchen boy' at the University of Oklahoma Biological Station, on Lake Texoma on the Oklahoma-Texas border. My duties were mostly to wash dishes, with occasional extras, such as potato-peeling. The job was unpaid but included room and board.

Why did I take on such drudgery? Because even at that tender age, we lads (at that time, there were no kitchen girls) were given time off from work if we wanted to sit in on university classes, unofficially as 'auditors'. On a space-available basis, we were allowed to join undergraduates and graduate students in lectures, laboratory exercises, and field trips. Some took up the offer, some did not, but I did so with enthusiasm.

The first summer I took 'Taxonomy of Vascular Plants', taught by a charismatic teacher, George Goodman, whose engaging attitude had much to do with the choice, as I'd had no previous interest in botany at all. We learned to use identification keys, sometimes requiring microscopic as well as macroscopic scrutiny, and memorised countless systematic terms and scientific names. We learned to press plant specimens for herbarium storage. Best of all, we went on field trips to ecotypes as diverse as humid riverine forests and arid scrublands to collect samples of their vegetation.

The second summer I took 'Field Entomology', taught by a more taciturn but no less welcoming professor, George Bick, a specialist on damselflies. Again, we learned the names of scores of insect orders and families, and how to collect and prepare specimens for museum collections. Also, there was a competitive aspect: Each of us was to make a personal collection, to be handed in at the end of the course, of as many taxonomic families in the Class Insecta as possible. Naturally, each of us students sought to get the most, and this involved more than just wandering around with insect nets, hoping to get lucky. For example, I secured and stashed away in the woods the left-over bodies of fishes dissected in the parasitology lab, hoping to get specimens of scavenging beetles. Others put out overnight feeding stations of sweetened water, in order to attract moths. We soon turned to swapping specimens, to our mutual advantage. It was great fun.

The third summer I took 'Herpetology', with the man who was to become one of my mentors, Charles Carpenter, who specialised in the behaviour of the lizard family Iguanidae (see **7, 10, 43, 54, 106**). These field trips were exciting, for Oklahoma offered at least five species of venomous snakes, along with frogs, salamanders, turtles, etc. The first experience of handling a copperhead or an eastern diamond-backed rattlesnake was adrenaline-pumping and unforgettable. This early exposure later led to field expeditions further afield, in Mexico (**9**) and the Bahamas (**12**), and eventually to scientific publications.

Whatever I've done as a scientist over a lifetime was based on such foundations and mentors.

6 BONES AND STONES

My first love was palaeontology, that is, fossils of plant and animal life. I spent hours in the Stovall Museum of Natural History at the University of Oklahoma, especially in the room that housed the mineralised bones of large amphibians, reptiles and mammals. To be frank, its compelling attraction was dinosaurs!

This led me to approach the University's vertebrate palaeontologist, David Kitts, to ask how I could join in dinosaur hunting. As I was only a boy, he let me down softly by telling me that Oklahoma didn't actually have the sediments to yield such fossils, but he offered to take me with him for a day trip to look for fossils at a quarry in the Arbuckle Mountains. True to his word, he pointed me to pockets in the limestone face where sediments yielded tiny fossils of mammals, no bigger than mice. What a thrill!

But what about *real* palaeontology? That had to wait decades, until I was a primatologist, and increasingly interested in the implications of studying living apes for the reconstruction of human evolutionary origins. This meant time spent in museums and caves in Europe and Africa. The most productive of my limited efforts came in western Kenya, around Lake Turkana, where many important human ancestors have been discovered. There I assisted in surface surveying and found fragmentary fossils of many creatures, mostly crocodiles and fish, but few mammals, and never primates. There was always hope: In those climes, fossils erode out after every major rainstorm, and very rarely, these yield important new discoveries.

The high point for me came in the related field of archaeology, just as I retired from academia. When visiting West Turkana, I was lucky enough to see the 'dig' site of Lomekwi 3, which had just revealed the oldest known stone tools. These primitive lithics were dated to 3.3 million years ago, pushing back the date of this key point in human evolution by 700,000 years. The only human ancestral forms around at that time had brains no bigger than the living African great apes!

I watched spellbound on the day that the first flaked core was recovered *in situ*. Another great thrill! Lest you get the wrong impression, my job that day was menial, that is, to write the coded numbers on tapes to be affixed to the finds, as they were assembled and boxed.

7 HERPS

Throughout my adolescence, I was fixated on amphibians and reptiles. Herpetology is the study of these two classes of vertebrates, hence the nickname 'herps'. These creatures were plentiful in those days, even in town, as tadpoles in ditches or lizards scurrying about the garden. I caught toads and lizards and housed them in terraria and kept salamanders in aquaria. They lived in my bedroom for close-up study. One of my projects, on the circadian rhythms of a small and obscure species of snake, got me to the semi-finals of the Westinghouse National Science Talent Search. That recognition yielded only a certificate, but it was reinforcing to a callow youth.

More importantly, I fell further under the influence of Prof. Charles Carpenter, a zoology professor at the University of Oklahoma, who let me join his field trips to capture lizards further afield than my home state. While still a teenager, I joined him and his students on trips to the deserts of the southwestern USA and northern Mexico (see **9**). I learned the skills of noosing, that is, using a long cane pole with a fishing-line lasso on the end to snag the animal around the neck or leg, without injury.

'Doc' Carpenter had a laboratory on the North Campus of the university, with large pens where the iguanid lizards could range and display to one another, and even mate and have offspring. As an undergraduate, my job as a part-time work-study student was to feed the many hungry reptilian mouths, mostly with live insects. In the warm months, I caught wild ones on the grounds by sweep-netting, and in the colder months, I maintained indoor colonies of meal-worms and moth larvae (which had to be fed too!) As most iguanid lizards take only moving prey, I also rolled canned dogfood into little balls no bigger than peas. These were released to accelerate down wooden ramps into the large enclosures, where they hit the ground and skimmed across the substrate, to be gobbled up by the pursuing lizards. Unusual job skills for a young man, but perhaps of limited transferability!

Much later in life, when people knew that I did field work in Africa, they often asked about my encounters with poisonous snakes (**54**). These occurred often and never led to problems for me, but twice others were badly bitten. At Bilenge, in the Mahale Mountains, working with Anthony Collins, we lived in a small fishing village on Lake Tanganyika. One of the fishermen, a young man in good health, was pulling in the gill-nets in the morning when he was unluckily bitten on the arm by a big water cobra. These aquatic snakes are fish-eaters which are attracted to fish thrashing around when caught in the nets. Usually the snakes have drowned by the time the nets are pulled in, but not this time. We'd left for the field before the fisherman went out and by the time we returned to the village in the evening, he was dead. Even if we had been there, we could not have helped, as we had no anti-venin and the nearest clinic was many hours away by boat.

Years later, when I was at the Koobi Fora research station on the eastern shore of Lake Turkana, in remote western Kenya, a young teaching assistant was bitten by a smaller cobra. It happened at night, when he was asleep in bed; the snake fell on top of him and in his efforts to repel it, it bit him on the arm. The snake had been in the rafters of the building, presumably hunting for birds or rodents. The rest of us were awakened by his cries for help. There was no anti-venin on site, but the station had an air strip and membership in the Flying Doctors, based in Nairobi. So far, so good, but the air strip was only minimal, an elongated, smooth clearing, with no lighting, so the Flying Doctors could not pick him up until dawn the next morning. Pairs of us took it in turns to stay up all night with him, trying to keep him awake and calm. He went into shock, but sometimes became animated and confused, perhaps even hallucinatory. At first light, we heard the sound of the approaching ambulance plane, which landed and whisked him away. He survived and had the resilience and gumption to return again the following year for another season at the station.

Many years later in retirement, I had time enough to return to data collected on herps while chasing chimpanzees. This led to published scientific journal articles on crocodiles, lizards and snakes, all in relation to the apes. A very satisfying full circle, and of course, I sent copies to Doc Carpenter!

McGrew WC (2015) Snakes as hazards: Modelling risk by chasing chimpanzees. *Primates* 56: 107-111.

McGrew WC (2015) Why don't chimpanzees eat monitor lizards? *African Primates* 10: 40-52.

8 NUMBERS GAMES

My whole pre-university education was at University School, part of the Department of Education, University of Oklahoma, for teacher training and educational research. Most of the permanent staff had university appointments, and many of the pupils were offspring of university faculty members. Thus, it was academically challenging.

However, a major constraint for sports was the school's small enrolment. Grades 9-12 (secondary) had fewer than 100 pupils in total, and my co-educational graduating class in 1962 numbered only 18. Also, 'Uni High' was unusual: Though a state school, it was perceived as elitist and snooty, and nicknamed by pupils at the public schools as 'Sissy High'. This status perhaps was exaggerated by all the other schools in the Canadian Valley Conference being rural, mostly farm kids, and we were the 'city slickers'.

The small enrolment numbers meant that we had not enough manpower to field a (gridiron) football team, which requires at least 11 players, and that absolute minimum would be vulnerable to injury or absence. Nor, in any given year, could we be sure to have enough able-bodied males for a baseball team, requiring at least nine players, so some years we competed in baseball but some years not.

Athletics and basketball were a different matter. Track and field is largely an individual sport (apart from relays), so no problem. A handful, even one committed individual, was enough. I ran sprints with middling success, but in retrospect, should have done longer distances. Basketball required only five players on court at a time, and so training sessions could be done with only 10. Thus, of necessity, basketball was our sporting focus, and luckily I was tall enough to be useful at it. The team did well, and sometimes we beat teams from schools with much larger enrolments, which was satisfying.

As an undergraduate, I continued to dabble in both sports, but gave studies top priority. Later, at Oxford as a postgraduate student, I could not resist returning to basketball, especially as another member of the incoming class of 1965 was Bill Bradley, a famous player who had set national scoring records at Princeton University. At the trials, we both made the team, which went on to win the English national championship. More importantly, we soundly defeated Cambridge in two Varsity Matches, and I left Oxford as a Double Blue. (see **22, 28**)

9 BILGE

My title here is a memorable acronym for 'Biology of the Insular Lizards of the Gulf Expedition', which was a spring vacation trip to desert islands in the Gulf of California (Sea of Cortez) to bring indigenous lizards back alive. The islands between mainland Mexico and Baja California really were *desert* isles, that is, devoid of fresh water, so uninhabited. There *was* bilge, as our vessel of transport on the high seas was a leaky, out-of-season shrimp boat, therefore available for hire, cheap. Hence occurred the most memorable scientific enterprise of my young career, in a party of 10, five professors and five student assistants (plus, of course, the boat's skeleton crew.) I was the youngest, just an impressionable teen-ager, assisting Doc Carpenter.

The Oklahoma-based academic party drove in two station-wagons to the port of Guaymas, on the west coast of Mexico. After some haggling, we hired the boat for two weeks, which necessarily involved provisions of food and water for the whole trip, from the outset. We then chugged from island to island, with a simple daily routine: anchor offshore in a quiet cove, row ashore in the early morning in a dinghy loaded with cages, split up into five parties of two, and get on with catching the lizards. The teams of two dispersed, as each sought a different kind of target: Some lizards, such as iguanids, could be noosed out in the open, while others, such as geckos, had to be winkled out of crevices in the rocks. At midday, we returned to the boat, sweaty and exhausted, for lunch and siesta, then went back out again later in the afternoon for another session. This worked fine.

The limitations of our chosen vessel became apparent as the days unfolded. It had no refrigeration system, just an icebox, so with each day the perishable foodstuffs 'ripened' in the heat, with much of it, especially meat, becoming inedible before even half the voyage had elapsed. Also, the volume of fresh water on board was enough for drinking and cooking, but not for bathing and washing clothes. So, we began to 'ripen' too, with only the sea breezes to keep us from being unbearably pungent.

So, what to do? After one of the professors, perhaps the most finicky one, threw all the rotten provisions overboard, we resorted to fishing on the journeys between islands. This proved surprisingly productive, so long as we were content to eat fish. For bathing, it seemed obvious that we should use the sea, as the waters there were crystal-clear and inviting. However, that clarity was important, as one of the crew had to climb the mast with a rifle to keep a sharp eye out for sharks. Whether this precaution would have been sufficient had a shark arrived was never tested. Either way we did not linger over our ablutions.

Time on board in transit was wondrous for us naturalists. At one point, 'flying fish' landed *en masse* on deck when a school of them was chased into the air by a predator. Bottle-nosed dolphins sometimes accompanied the boat, peering up at us as they easily maintained pace beside it. Their most impressive feat was to surface and dive across the prow just in front of it as we sped along, apparently competing to see who could cut it the closest without being churned under. Evenings were made more convivial by a rationed supply of beer that was consumed at sundown. Of course, it was warm, but so what?

Once back in port, mission accomplished, we loaded up the station wagons with cages and headed back north to the USA. The last cage put on board each vehicle contained a couple of rattlesnakes, as Doc Carpenter had found on previous trips that customs checks proceeded more quickly at the border when such a cage was the first thing to be encountered by customs officials.

10 FIRST PUBLICATION

My first scientific paper emerged in 1963, when I was 19 years old, as an unexpected by-product of a summer job. I had worked then as a field assistant, between leaving high school and starting university, for the Oklahoma Fisheries Research Laboratory. Our crew did a pre-impoundment survey of the watershed to be included in the making of a huge reservoir, which became Lake Eufala, in eastern Oklahoma. Our job was to sample fish from rivers and streams, using a variety of techniques, from netting to electric shocking, which yielded many dead fish.

As we were on the road, moving from place to place, staying only a few days in each bivouac, we lived hand to mouth. Often for supper we cooked the fish caught that day, after identifying, measuring and weighing them. Moreover, when local farmers learned of our presence in the area, they came round with garden produce to swap for fresh fish. Thus, we had the fruit and veg to go with our fishy suppers.

One evening, when I was cleaning fish for supper, I slit open a bulging channel catfish to find that its stomach was full of eight hatchling diamond-backed water snakes! The predatory fish must have eaten a clutch of these newly-hatched snakes not long before we caught it. Everyone was astonished, as the combined length of the snakes was much greater than that of the fish.

Later I looked at the published scientific literature on the topic of fish eating reptiles and could find no previous cases reported. So I wrote up a short natural history note, with a view to submitting it for publication to *Copeia*, the recognised journal of the American Society of Ichthyologists and Herpetologists. Of course, I asked a senior scientist to check my manuscript and he made a few corrections.

Only later, when the article appeared in print, did I realise that I'd made a very basic and stupid mistake. Being then unfamiliar with the metric system, I'd confused millimetres and centimetres, so that the swallowed fish were 'minimised' by a factor of 10, more like earthworms than snakes. I waited for the criticism that would flood in, destroying my scientific career before it even started. But it never happened, which probably means that no one ever read it.

McGrew WC (1963) Channel catfish feeding on diamond-backed water snakes. *Copeia* 1963:178-179.

11 POLITICAL SCHEMES

In the summer before I graduated from high school, my school sent me to a summer camp run by the American Legion (a powerful American veterans' organisation). There we were propagandised in semi-military style, though I recall spending most of my time playing basketball. One of the books given to each participant was FBI director J. Edgar's Hoover's *Masters of Deceit*, about how communists seek to take over the world. One chapter outlined the commie technique of clandestinely taking over an organisation by sneaky but legal procedures.

Two years later, as a first-year university student, I was elected to an honorary society, Phi Eta Sigma, for males who had achieved a certain standard of grades in their studies. At the first meeting of the group, we were to elect five officers (president, vice-president, treasurer, etc.). Superimposed on this procedure was fierce competition within the group among the social fraternities ('frats') to which many of the members belonged. That is, each frat sought to get its men elected, through solidarity as a voting bloc, so that, for example, Sigma Chi individual 'A' would nominate Sigma Chi individual 'B', and all would vote as a block, hoping to win the election. Unfortunately, the strategy was obvious and so doomed to failure, as all present quickly could see what they were up to. (With advance planning, coalitions could have been formed, and reciprocal arrangements made, but no one seemed to have thought of that.)

Instead, following Hoover, I suggested an alternative strategy to my Delta Tau Delta classmates, that we go to the meeting individually. Once there each of us would seek out a friend in the group, preferably one who was not a fraternity member. Then he was to ask the friend to nominate him for the office being voted upon. So when a non-frat guy nominated one of us Delts on his own, no one else saw any signs of frat solidarity. (Of course, we'd agreed in advance which office each of us would go for, so as not to stand against one another.) The major frat blocks voted predictably or chaotically and in effect cancelled each other out, leaving the way open for us apparently unattached individuals to win the elections.

When the dust settled, we Delts had won four of the five offices, following Hoover's unintended tutelage on how to subvert an organisation. So much for town-meeting democracy, at least with naïve youths.

12 SEEKING CURLY-TAILS

As an undergraduate, I did part-time work-study in a breeding colony of iguanid lizards. My duties as a keeper were mostly feeding and cleaning, but it gave me time to get to know 'Doc' Carpenter better (7). At one point we discussed his ambition to assemble a colony of all the world's iguanids, so he could compare the courtship displays of the males. He already had been to the Galapagos and brought back the biggest members of that family, marine iguanas. He mentioned that among the few species lacking was a curly-tailed lizard, endemic to the island of Bimini, in the Bahamas. Spontaneously, I volunteered to go get them for him.

Of course, such an expedition required money, but he had a big NSF grant. Doc was wise enough to stipulate that although he would pay half of the costs, I had to raise the other half through grant-getting (not just by dunning the parents!) So, in 1965, at age 20 years, I wrote my first research grant application, for $200, and luckily, it came through.

Flying commercially was easy enough from Oklahoma to Miami, but how to get to Bimini? The answer was by seaplane, from Miami Beach. I was the only passenger when we rolled down the ramp on wheels, then into the water, on pontoons, to take off from Biscayne Bay. Wow!

I was hosted on Bimini by the Lerner Marine Laboratory of the American Museum of Natural History. Doc had supplied all the equipment, including cages, to bring 'em back alive. Having been on previous lizard-catching expeditions to Mexico, I already knew the techniques, which here meant noosing, so,

I was set. Only one problem, I couldn't find the lizards. Day after day, I searched fruitlessly. I found other lizards, but no curly-tails. My visit was passing and it was beginning to get embarrassing. Then, by chance, a fisherman told me where to find them, on unlikely looking sand spits offshore. Sensing my enthusiasm (relief?), he offered to take me across in his boat. The place was crawling with them! So, in the nick of time, things had worked out. Thank goodness!

When I was packing up, the night before returning home, an employee of the lab brought me a sack which turned out to contain a Bimini boa, an endemic species of snake. He presented it as a going-away gift, but I had no appropriate cage for her, as she was many times the size of the small lizards. I considered just waiting a bit and then releasing her, but I didn't want to insult my hosts, so I coiled her up like a piece of rope into one of the tiny lizard compartments, hoping for the best. (Boas are notably docile.) (see **106**).

Follow-up: I got back to Norman with nary a casualty, and the lizards settled in nicely and produced many young. The snake also weathered the journey and was given to the Oklahoma City Zoo, making them the only zoo in the USA to have the species. As a *lagniappe* (unexpected bonus), it turned out that she was already gravid, so she too produced many young.

13 HOW TO GET A RHODES SCHOLARSHIP

The phrase 'a life-changing experience' is over-used but is sometimes accurate. That is so here. Winning a Rhodes Scholarship in October, 1964, changed my life, in ways that I could not have imagined. I would not be here in Scotland, 50+

years later, writing this memoir, were it not for that event. It came about only because I was blessed by lots of good luck.

Growing up in post-war Oklahoma, in a small state college town, I had no known links to the United Kingdom of Great Britain and Northern Ireland, nor could I imagine ever having any (**23**). As a child, I'd had a pen pal in Stoke on Trent, but it didn't last long. Of course, I knew of Rhodes Scholarships and Oxford, but in a vague, almost mythical sense, as being accessible only to the academic elite, perhaps being the English equivalent to the USA's Ivy League. So I was surprised, in my second year of undergraduate study at the University of Oklahoma, to be invited to meet with Dr Savoie Lottinville, director of the University of Oklahoma Press. After a bit of small talk, he asked if I would be interested in applying for the Scholarship. He had been a Rhodes Scholar and had won a Blue in Boxing. I learned this because he asked about my sporting interests, and although I mentioned basketball and track and field, he asked me if I'd ever thought about playing rugby. I had not. That is all that I can recall of the conversation, but he urged me to get in touch with the two other former Rhodes Scholars in Norman, John Luttrell and Charles Springer. They urged me to apply to their college at Oxford, Merton, so I did. The seed was planted. The first lucky break…

Another lucky break came from a different direction. My mentor was Doc Carpenter, who my sparked my interest in studying animal behaviour in nature. He was an admirer of the Dutch ethologist Prof. Nikolaas Tinbergen (who later won a Nobel Prize), and he devoted a semester's seminar to the research of Tinbergen and his students. I was bitten by the ethology bug. Tinbergen was in the University of Oxford's

Department of Zoology, which was a convenient coincidence. In a moment of optimism, I wrote to him, asking if he would take me on as a PhD student, if I got a Rhodes Scholarship. After exchanging a few letters, he agreed (which later turned out to be important). Yet another lucky break.

In the autumn of 1964, I applied. The selection process had three stages: first, the University of Oklahoma held an on-campus competition to see who would represent it at the next level. I have no memories of this, so I suspect it was nothing extraordinary. Second, candidates from colleges and universities attended by Oklahomans were assembled in Oklahoma City to pick the two men to represent the state at the third level. There we in-staters were joined by other Oklahomans who were studying outside the state, as eligibility came via either route. I recall being a bit daunted by these guys from 'back east' who had come back to the state for this round. Because I was not yet taking seriously the possibilities of success, I just turned up and answered the questions put to me at interview.

Two of us were selected to represent Oklahoma. My counterpart was Gary Hassman, who besides having an impressive academic record, was a starter on the Oklahoma State University basketball team. More importantly, he was a state hero, because of a single incident. One day in the OSU changing room, his teammate, Bob Swaffer, impatiently stuck his arm into a still-spinning towel compactor, which ripped it off. He collapsed in shock, but Gary had the presence of mind to wrap the arm in towels and immerse it in ice water, while waiting for the ambulance to arrive. In hospital, the arm was re-attached successfully. Bob never played basketball again, but he had his arm back. This was the first successful such medical procedure, and it made worldwide news. Gary was the first to admit that this might have helped his chances a bit in the competition.

We were told to report to the third and decisive final stage of the Rhodes competition, the regional finals, in New Orleans, Louisiana. Then the USA Rhodes competition was divided into eight regions of 6-7 states each; Oklahoma was in the Gulf Region, comprising Alabama, Arkansas, Louisiana, Mississippi, Oklahoma, and Texas. Nationwide, 32 scholars would be selected, that is, four from each region. Ours was thought to be perhaps the weakest region in which to compete, given the reputed low level of higher education in the Deep South, compared with the rest of the country, such as New England. Another lucky break?

I chose to fly from Oklahoma City to New Orleans, but had never been in an airplane before. When I went to the travel agent to book a ticket, she asked if I wanted to fly Coach or First Class? I thought: the Rhodes Trust is such a prestigious organisation that they surely would expect us to fly first class; to do otherwise might be embarrassing or even insulting to them. (It remains the first and only time in my life that I ever have bought a first class air ticket.) I was oblivious to my profligacy, even when I later turned in my expenses claim and some eyebrows were raised. (Later I heard that this had never happened before.) But, being a classy bunch, the Rhodes folks never said a word, and I was reimbursed. Lucky again!

The appointed hotel was in the French Quarter of New Orleans, and it was imposing, clearly a high-dollar establishment. Guests were greeted out of a taxi by a black doorman who looked to be seven feet tall, wearing a sort of Napoleonic uniform. In the evening, we assembled for a welcoming reception consisting of drinks and canapés, to acquaint the committee members and candidates. It was a bit nerve-racking as we applicants sized one another up. Most seemed to be from private colleges or universities, with manners to match, so not much ice was broken, at least for this Oklahoma boy. The reception ended early, after we were given the schedule for the next day's interviewing.

Most of the candidates said that they would retire to their rooms to get a good night's sleep, but others admitted that they would be cramming for the interview by reading up on current events. They had their copies of *Time* and *Newsweek* at hand. I was about to follow suit, but Gary proposed otherwise. Based on the fact that we were two young men in New Orleans for the first time, on a Friday night, and that this might never happen again, he proposed that we hit the town.

Astonishing myself, I agreed to this. We headed to Bourbon Street, which was raucous and garish. I have only fragmentary recollections of the evening, but one memory will give a flavour of it. We sat at a table at the front of a strip club, only a few feet from the 'exotic dancer', who caught Gary's eye, and perhaps to see if his eyes would bulge any wider, oriented her tassled breasts to him and wiggled them, each one alternately and independently. Amazing! Such were the learning opportunities in the Big Easy in those days. I rationalised the whole experience by telling myself that this distraction would keep me from worrying myself into insomnia in my hotel room. Yet another lucky break?

Next morning, when I came down the hotel stairs to the

dining room, by chance I met one of the committee members, headed the same way. After a mutually awkward moment, he invited me to join him for breakfast. No one else came along, so we ate and chatted, just the two of us. I regret that I cannot recall his name, but he was a family doctor from Mississippi. We talked about all sorts of things, including animal behaviour.

I remember little of the interview, which seems to be a common response to the stress of such a situation. It lasted about 30 minutes, and if anyone had asked me afterwards, I'd have had no clue as to how well I'd done. I recall telling them of my correspondence with Tinbergen, which seemed to impress them. What did transpire was that the Mississippi physician was the person who led my interview. (I later learned that each committee member was given advance responsibility for leading the interviews of a couple of candidates.) Some of the questions he asked me were based on our morning conversation! So, I had got unbelievably lucky in making the simple decision of when to go to breakfast.

When the interviewing was finished, we were eventually called together and girded ourselves to hear the results. The chairman said that they could not yet reach a decision, and so they would be re-interviewing some of the candidates. I was not re-interviewed, which of course could mean either one might be safely in the bag or already decidedly out of it. So the rest of us were sent away to wait some more; it seemed like hours.

Finally we re-assembled, and the chairman announced the four winners, which he said would be read out in alphabetical order by surname. First, Thomas Cotton (Stanford University).

Then William Keach (University of Texas). Then Timothy Vanderver (Washington and Lee College). My heart sank. Then, he said something like, "Oh, sorry, I got that out of order. William McGrew, University of Oklahoma." I was truly floored, unable to take it in.

So, how many lucky breaks had it taken to get to that point? Enough it seems.

ADULTHOOD

14 OCEAN LINING

When I went to Oxford in 1965, aged 21 years, to begin postgraduate study, air travel across the Atlantic had certain constraints. Landings to refuel in Newfoundland or Iceland were still common when faced with strong headwinds. Rhodes Scholars got around that problem, as by tradition they travelled together from the USA to the UK by ship, as a way of getting to know one another, before arriving in Oxford and dispersing to their colleges.

So the American portion of the Rhodes class of 1965 had to decide to which line to give our business, and a committee was selected to investigate the options, which were American, British, French or Italian, at the highest level. Each of these companies had big ocean liners with all the bells and whistles, regularly plying back and forth between New York and Europe.

Each had its pros and cons, for example, the SS *United States* was the fastest, doing the journey directly in only five days. The SS *France* was reputed to have the best food. In the end we chose Cunard Lines, and so the *Queen Mary*, which took an extra day, as it stopped in Cherbourg en route. Thus, my first footfall in Europe was in France!

She was a venerable ship, with a proud history. In WWII, she had served as a troop ship taking American soldiers to Europe. She was all metal and wood, no plastic, and 110% British in every way. As a group, we could negotiate a deal. We chose first-class cabins but second-class dining. Why? Because first-class dining required formal, black tie dressing up every evening, which seemed a bit much. (I owned none of the required clothing). At our first evening meal, I was impressed by the sophistication of the Ivy League scholars, with their knowledge of wines. It was my first time to drink wine, ever, but an anticipatory event. (see **66, 67**)

So, what to do with six days at sea? Pre-satellite, we were essentially cut off from the outside world, reliant only on a daily mimeographed news sheet issued by the company, with snippets of current events reported. There was a cinema, but it showed few films, and by halfway across, I'd seen them all. So, we did a lot of reading and drinking. Learning about British beer was easy, as there are no taxes or tariffs on the high seas, so a pint of bitter cost only two shillings and two pence.

Today, Rhodes Scholars still assemble in New York for a 'Sailing Dinner', in fact a whole weekend of activities, before heading out to JFK airport to board a flight to Heathrow. Perhaps they still negotiate a group rate, but they miss out on the extended, enforced socialising, aided and abetted by ethanol. Meanwhile, the *Queen Mary* retired long ago from cruising and sits in regal retirement, moored in Long Beach, California. It now serves as a floating hotel and conference centre. I visited her once and was pleasantly surprised by how much of her original ambience has been retained. I swear I still could detect the faint odour of brass polish…

15 THE LORD OF THE RINGS HIMSELF

Soon after our arrival in Oxford in 1965, Merton College gave us new postgraduate students a matriculation dinner. It was the only time in three years there that I ever sat at Merton's high table, so it was an opportunity to be made the most of. We were seated alternately, students and Fellows, all of the latter being new persons to us. Afterwards, some of us went to the nearby Northgate pub, to exchange reports of the evening's happenings over pints of beer. Most of the comments were predictable and not so interesting, as in: "I sat next to the Saville Professor of Moral Hagiography and didn't understand a word of what he said", or "I chatted all evening with a professor of mathematics but couldn't ask him a single intelligent question about his work." *Et cetera.*

When it came to me for my turn, I said something like: "I can't report much because the Fellow across from whom I was seated didn't say much at all. He seemed to expect me to have some questions, for him, but of course I didn't. How could I, given that he was a stranger?" Then someone asked who he was. I could only reply, "His name was unusual, something like Tollkeen." At this point, there was a collective gasp, then much laughter. What an ignoramus I was!

Yes, JRR Tolkien was then the Professor of English Language and Literature and a Fellow of Merton College, and he already had written his famous books.

16 SKIING BEHIND THE IRON CURTAIN

In 1967, my wife and I decided to learn to ski, or rather, to ski on snow as opposed to water, which we already knew how to do from growing up in Oklahoma. It seemed obvious that we should go to the Alps, to Austria or Switzerland, but we quickly learned that the famous ski resorts were out of our price range. By chance, we found a flyer for a student-run trip to Poland, for skiing in the Carpathian Mountains, and its cost, all-inclusive of transport, accommodation, and skiing equipment, was remarkably low. I now suspect that it was somehow 'subsidised' by who knows who.

We signed up for round-trip rail travel from London to Zakopane, a ski resort, via Warsaw and Krakow. Instructions for the trip were straightforward, except for a paragraph that urged us to take along some small things to give to our Polish hosts, as this was the custom in that country. This idea sounded charming, but we were puzzled by the suggested gifts, such as women's tights, throw-away razors, and even blue jeans. We complied and did so, as naïve European travellers.

The journey took us across the Channel by ferry, and eventually into Germany. It was the height of the Cold War, so we expected an adventure and were a bit nervous. At the frontier, entering East Germany, the border guards were stereotypically stern but polite. We had to fill in various forms, including an accounting of how much cash we had with us, in all currencies, but we were soon on our way. Berlin whizzed by and soon we were in Poland, with a warmer populace, so we relaxed.

In Warsaw, we picked up our skiing equipment, rented

from the university there, and the first problem arose. Despite having booked in advance ski boots for my foot size, none was available, so I had to accept a pair that scrunched up my toes. In Krakow, we stopped for lunch in the beautiful city square, completely rebuilt after its destruction in WWII. Finally, we arrived in Zakopane, which looked like a ski resort should, except perhaps a bit dowdy, by unfair comparison with Zermatt or Chamonix.

Our guide suggested that we go to the bank to exchange pounds into zlotys, but to limit ourselves to a small amount, say, 10 pounds. This seemed like a frugal amount, but we complied, and duly pocketed the official exchange receipt. Soon all became clear. The 'gifts' that we had brought for friendly relations with the locals were to be sold quietly to them, on the black market. Who knew that Levis could be so prized? Furthermore, the unofficial (black market) rate of exchange was *much* more generous than the official one at the bank. We were set to live far beyond our usual student budget!

On the slopes, it became clear on the first day that downhill skiing with flexed toes pressed against the boot was a non-starter. It would have been hard enough acquiring new skills without enduring constant pain. So for me, daily *après ski* started early and carried on for longer than normal, buoyed up by my pocket-full of zlotys. If you are wondering how these informal currency exchanges took place, it was like this: in a public place, often a bar, a stranger would approach you, and say something in Polish or broken English that included the word 'zloty'. You two then would quietly exit and slip behind the building, where you would write the amount of your available pounds in the snow, then he would write his offered exchange rate as well, and if you both were agreeable, you exchanged currency and wiped away the snow. Simple, especially if you were totally naïve and never stopped to consider that this might be a police sting.

Good times were there to be had, especially with money to spare, though for me not on the slopes. I brought two exquisite filigreed wooden plates, which still hang on my wall. One evening we enjoyed a horse-drawn sleigh ride, lit by torchlight, over snowy hill and vale. The sleighs even had jingle bells. Soon the week was over, and we packed to go home, our luggage now filled with souvenirs, some quite expensive, replacing the gifts that we'd brought.

As we approached the East German border, on our rail journey home, we realised the problem. How could we account for all our holiday purchases, if we still had most of the pounds with which we'd entered the country? We could hide the currency in our shoes or some such ploy, but what if they searched us? More of a problem was having only one bank receipt for a measly 10 pounds, so how could we have afforded to buy all the goodies? Oops. The border guards showed no interest. Whew!

17 FRONT PAGE NEWS

In 1965, when I took up a Rhodes Scholarship at Oxford, the war in Vietnam was heating up, at least for Americans. (It was already hot enough for Southeast Asians.) Many of my fellow scholars were reading Politics, Philosophy and Economics (PPE) as a major degree subject, so many heated discussions occurred among us. Coming from Oklahoma, a conservative southwestern state, I was not used to such debate, but like others, I came to realise that I could not support the war. We had many conversations about what (if anything) to do about it.

Eventually, someone proposed, probably infused by an extra-high level of hubris, that we should write a joint letter to the *New York Times*, asking penetrating questions to President Lyndon Johnson about the war. Several of the class of 31 scholars demurred, mostly those who had the foresight to see that this might negatively affect their future political ambitions, but I signed. At that early stage of the war, the letter seemed a notable step, although later, of course, as opposition to the war grew, it looked absolutely wimpy. I guess we envisioned it appearing on the letters-to-the-editor page, having registered our dissent in passing. Imagine our surprise when it appeared on the front page of the *NYT*, as well as being accompanied by an editorial on the inside of the newspaper.

Apparently, media in every state that had current Rhodes Scholars in residence then wanted to know if their boys had signed up. Oklahomans on the whole did not approve of such an unpatriotic act, and it later was a chicken that came back to roost for me. (**18, 19**) It was the only time in my life that I ever made the front page news for anything!

18 VIETNAM

Having been born in 1944, I was 21 years old in 1965, when President Johnson upped the USA's involvement in the war between the North and South Vietnamese. I was in just the right age-range to be drafted into the US Army to go and fight. Eventually, I was classified as 1-A, being the top level of the ranked list of eligibility for the draft.

However, I was opposed to the war and was active in anti-war activities both in the USA and in the UK. In 1966, I joined other Rhodes Scholars in signing a letter of protest to Johnson, news coverage of which made the front page of the *New York Times*. In 1968, I took part in the biggest anti-war demonstration in the UK, the protest rally at the American embassy in Grosvenor Square. (**19**) So when the Army's call to report for military medical examination came, I pondered what to do.

In the end, I opted for exile, that is, to cast my future with the UK, hoping that they would not extradite me to the USA. I made a final trip to Oklahoma, gathered what precious belongings I could carry, closed my modest bank account, and said my goodbyes. Unlike Canada, which had a welcoming policy toward draft resisters, the UK did not, so there was a risk involved.

However, the expected call-up did not happen. Acting on a hunch, my father (who as an army veteran supported the war) asked me for my legal power of attorney, which I gave, and went along to the local draft board in Norman, Oklahoma. There he asked to see my file, which was a legal right, where he discovered, much to his and my surprise, that they had been keeping records of my anti-war activities, including newspaper cuttings, etc. This was evidence of prejudicial victimisation and highly illegal, and my father had caught them red-handed, making any attempt to draft me unlikely to succeed. He made clear that if they did so, we would see them in court, and that finished that. Blood is thicker than water, thank goodness.

19 GROSVENOR SQUARE

In 2018 came the 50th anniversary of a notable event, the mass demonstration against the Vietnam war which terminated in confrontation at the American Embassy in this normally staid square in London. After a rally in Hyde Park, tens of thousands of demonstrators flowed in rivers of protest, converging on the square. Problems arose when police tried to stop this influx from the various side-streets as the square filled up to bursting. Eventually, only a thin space in front of the embassy, which took up all of one side of the square, was unoccupied by the demonstrators, kept at bay by a line of mounted police.

My memories are as chaotic as the occasion, but here are a couple of them. When my wave of protesters reached the square, coming in from a side-street, we were confronted by a line of bobbies stretching across the street, seeking to deny us access. We paused momentarily, then spontaneously linked arms and charged forward. This decision happened without consultation or appeals among ourselves, as most of us were complete strangers to one another. It was true and instant collective action. Our combined force was unstoppable, and we burst through the police rank and into the square. The feeling was one of total exhilaration! (In those days, police did not have riot shields, or use tear gas, rubber bullets, or water cannons. All that came later and doubtless would have made a difference then.)

Later, having worked my way closer to the front, I began to appreciate for the first time how *big* horses are. There was a good reason for keeping space between them and us, at bay. Folks pushing from the back inevitably caused those at the front to inch forward, and at some invisible point, that forward movement triggered police action. The line of mounted horses surged forward in a cavalry-like charge, straight into the crowd. It was terrifying, as people tried to avoid being trampled. Most succeeded but not all. I was lucky, as by the time the horses reached me, their momentum had been slowed by the mass of humanity into which they ploughed.

Of course, I do not blame the horses, but I've never looked at one in quite the same way since. (34)

20 DYLAN, ETC

In 1966, in my first year at Oxford, a group of us decided to go down to London to see Bob Dylan perform on stage in the venerable Royal Albert Hall. It was his first trip to the UK, and many were curious to see in person this emerging musician. He was then in transition from folk singer to rocker, and many of the fans of the former were not happy about the latter. Once we got to the venue, it was clear that we were not the only ones who were curious. It was packed, sold out; we stood in the throng on the ground floor. More impressively, the boxes above us were filled with familiar celebrity faces, such as the Rolling Stones. Apparently, they were curious too.

Dylan solved the problem in two halves. In the first half of the performance, he played alone and stuck to rhythm guitar and harmonica, playing some folky favourites, such as Woody Guthrie's songs, and his own. After the interval, he switched to electric guitar and was joined by others, singing the songs that were to make him famous. It was magically memorable. I heard Dylan play twice more, once in Glasgow, Scotland, and once in Oxford, Ohio, at Miami University. Each time was notably different, as he kept evolving.

Over the decades I've heard live many other musicians, as varied as Herb Alpert, Mary Chapin Carpenter, Ray Charles, Leonard Cohen, Lyle Lovett, Willie Nelson, Tammy Wynette, etc. My all-time favourites are Runrig, a Scottish folk-rock group from the Western Isles, who sang in both English and Gaelic. I heard them several times, but the most memorable was their final concert in 2018, Day of Days, being the 30th anniversary of their modest start in the Outer Hebrides. Seventeen thousand tickets sold out on the first day, so they sold another 17,000 for their encore the next day. The setting was the grounds at the foot of Stirling Castle, looming in the background. Who do most regret not hearing in person? Eva Cassidy and Kris Kristofferson (Rhodes Scholar!)

None of these performers could have imagined that Dylan would someday become the Nobel Laureate in Literature!

21 FOOTBALL CONVERSION

One day in the summer of 1966, during my first year at Oxford, I was passing through London's Paddington railway station. In the main concourse, a small, temporary kiosk was selling something. I stopped to look, and it turned out to have tickets on sale for something called the World Cup, a forthcoming international football competition. I had heard of soccer but never seen it, so I asked about buying tickets. In the end, I bought one for the semi-final, having pondered whether I could afford to pay 17 shillings and 6 pence, or the lesser price of 12 shillings and 6 pence. (There were 20 shillings to a pre-decimal pound, so in today's metric terms, the ticket choice was 87 versus 64 pence.) Prudently, I opted for the cheaper ones. After all, that was a lot of money and I might not like this strange round-ball game.

On the allotted day, I went down to London to Wembley Stadium. By lucky chance, the semi-final match featured England against Portugal. Upon emerging from the stairwell to the crowd area, my mind was blown. Over 100,000 singing and shouting fans, standing and waving banners, were creating a deafening din. It was impossible not to be swept up in the fervour, and as the match unfolded with England doing well, it only got more so. For the record, Bobby Charlton scored two goals, and Nobby Stiles effectively neutralised the opposition's star player, Eusebio. It was an instant conversion experience for me.

Alas, I was shortly to leave for Israel to play in an international basketball tournament and so would be out of the UK on the day of the final, England vs. Germany. (**22**) Our team was dominated by Americans, who cared little for this type of football, so the captain scheduled a practice session at the time of the big game. So, while the rest of the world was glued to their television sets, we were training, but the English players kept disappearing off-court for long toilet breaks. It turned out that they had obtained and secreted a transistor radio, to which they sneaked away in rotation, to follow the progress of the match. England won, 4-2, for their only success so far in this competition. The next morning, the headline in the national English-language newspaper, the *Jerusalem Post*, was a simple: 'Thank You England'.

22 HAUNTING VOICES

In 1966, I played on a joint Oxford-Cambridge basketball team representing the United Kingdom that went to Israel to play in the International Universities Basketball Tournament. In our group were University of Kentucky (USA), University of Saloniki (Greece), and University of Heidelberg (West Germany). When we played the former, I was assigned to guard Pat Riley, who ended up in the USA's Professional Basketball Hall of Fame, thus a clear case of basking in reflected glory.

Our match against Heidelberg was played outdoors at night in Tel Aviv. When our bus arrived at the stadium, we noticed that there was a notable police presence, including mounted officers. We were curious to see the Germans, who for some reason had not been in the opening ceremony. It was during warm-ups that we realised that something unusual was happening. Much of the crowd were chanting in low but insistent voices, not like the usual cheering that we were used to at other sporting events. At first, we could not make out what was being said, then someone realised and a frisson went down my spine.

The crowd was chanting, slowly but pointedly and

emphatically, the names of concentration camps, "Auschwitz", "Buchenwald", "Dachau", etc, over and over again. It was chilling.

We won the game, but we will never know how much our opponents' play was affected by the crowd's actions. Their players never gave any sign of upset, and the game proceeded normally. Later, we found out that they were the first German team of any type to have played in a sporting contest in Israel after the war. They were guinea pigs, in a sense, as the organisers figured that young people who had not even been born before WWII might be greeted acceptably, if grudgingly, in Israel. However, the organisers had also figured that to have them join in the opening ceremony, entering the arena behind a German flag, would have been too much. They were probably right.

23 MCGREW ORIGINS

After getting a Rhodes Scholarship, but before I left the USA for England, I was contacted by a distant cousin, Ida Osterloh, who asked me to look into the McGrew family's origins in the British Isles. She'd done lots of research on the family after their arrival in the USA, in 1734, in Lancaster Co., Pennsylvania, but was stymied about where and when they'd come from on the other side of the Atlantic. (Recall that the 1960s were pre-web times, so all such research was based on paper records, which was tedious and time-consuming.) She had bits and pieces of clues, one from Northern Ireland (Ulster), being an isolated parish record from Co. Tyrone, the other being a minimal reference to MacGregors in Argyll in Scotland.

McGrew is one of the many septs of the Clan MacGregor, necessary after the clan name was proscribed by the London-based King James I (England) and VI (Scotland). My Scottish ancestors moved to Northern Ireland after the English victory in 1690 in the Battle of the Boyne, along with many other Protestant emigrants. My given name is common down the generations of our family, for 'King Billy' (William of Orange). You can find my namesake William McGrew, a soldier in the Scots Guards, killed in World War I, in the Roll of Honour in Edinburgh Castle.

As it happened, I was due to take part in an academic conference in Belfast, so I decided to take time off to do some sleuthing. In Belfast, the Registry Office had little of use, but the family name was listed on a paupers' roll from Tyrone. A helpful clerk there suggested that I go to Tyrone's county town, Omagh, where there might be local records. He recommended starting at the local newspaper office. So we rented a car and set off.

The office of the *Tyrone Constitution* was on the town's main street, easily found. As I entered the building, I glanced at a rack of time-cards, where employees clocked in and out of work. Amazingly, one of the cards was labelled with our surname! I asked to see the employee, and soon a pleasant young man came forward from the back and introduced himself. It was a funny feeling to say to a stranger, "You and I may well be long-lost cousins". He suggested that I should meet with his grandmother and her brother, who knew more about family history than anyone else.

Off we went to their modest home, where we were treated with warmth and welcome. I got out Mrs Osterloh's papers and they got out the family bible. Extraordinarily, when we worked back through the generations in both sets of records, they matched up at the right time. That is, the family that left Ulster was the same one that arrived in Pennsylvania! Thus, the long-lost link was re-stored, to the happy surprise of both parties. It is *possible* that all the McGrews (an uncommon surname) in North America are descended from this one family of immigrants.

24 HIBS FOREVER

When I arrived in Edinburgh in the summer of 1968, one of the first questions I heard from locals was: "Are you Hibs or Hearts?" I had no idea what they were talking about, but I soon learned that these were the two big Edinburgh football teams, Hibernian Football Club and Heart of Midlothian Football Club. Of course, I refer to the spherical form of ball, and therefore not rugby or gridiron. Apparently, one had to choose between these two arch-rivals.

By chance I fell in with a Hibs crowd, so my allegiance was decided. Fifty-plus years later, it remains. I still go along to Easter Road, their stadium, in Leith, wearing my green and white scarf, and in the winter, my green and white stocking cap, and in the summer my green and white replica strip, of which I have several, as they change every season. Others things have changed over the decades…

In 1968, most of the stands were uncovered and unseated. One stood with only the sky above, from start to finish. The place for a young man to be was on the east terrace, which was a concrete-covered slope of low steps, nothing more. There you stood among your fellow supporters, rain or shine. Scottish football plays throughout the winter, unlike most of Europe, which has a sensible winter shut-down. At Easter Road, it could be bitterly cold when the wind swept in from the Firth of Forth, so it was good for thermoregulation to be packed in like sardines. The heated language probably helped too.

There were no tickets or assigned places, just a mass of humanity (99% male). With a full house, this meant that you were surrounded by others and could hardly move. If you needed to excuse yourself, whether to get food or drink or to relieve yourself, you had to squeeze your way through the crowd to exit. Food consisted of Scotch pies, which were filled with all the parts of the cow (or other mammal) that the butchers otherwise could not sell. They were served hot, to be eaten by hand, so the fat ran down your wrist and congealed on your forearm. No alcohol was served, so the main drink sold was Bovril, a salty beef broth. The toilets were few and spartan, fine for urination but not for defecation.

What if you needed to pee, desperately, in the midst of that crowd (which was likely, see below)? That problem was solved by the empty drink containers at your feet, the result of folks having smuggled in pockets full of beer cans or bottles. The empties piled up on the steps at your feet so they could be used to urinate into. Of course, for the solution to work, your aim had to be true. Woe to the guy who watered the trouser-leg of the man in front! Also, whenever a goal was scored, everyone jumped up and down in celebration, which inadvertently tipped over these containers. Thus, by the end of an exciting match, the terraces flowed with pale yellow streams. We wore boots to the matches, not sandals.

If you wonder why this emphasis on urination, know that it was obligatory to drink multiple pints of beer at the pub before walking down the London Road to the ground. My favourite is the Theatre Royal, at the head of Leith Walk. Equally, it was necessary to repeat this pub-going ritual after the match, win or lose, for post-match analysis.

Today all has changed. We now sit in numbered seats beneath cover. We can easily go to the concession stands for a range of drinks and food. The men's room has an entrance and exit, through which we can pass easily and in an orderly manner. We wear normal shoes. Women and children are welcome. We listen more to recorded music than sing our own. So, we have evolved to relative gentility, but I wonder how memorable all this will be to today's young folks?

25 CHANGING ADDICTIONS

I took up distance running at age 41 years out of desperation, to try to quit smoking cigarettes. Having failed to quit using all the usual methods, I needed something else in order to succeed. I had read that distance running was addictive, because of a heightened sense of awareness caused by endorphins, called 'runner's high'. Perhaps that was the solution, to replace one addiction with another, healthier one? Only once before in my life had I run for more than a few hundred metres, as a teenager in a one-off road-race of three miles from Willis, Oklahoma to the University of Oklahoma Biological Station.

(5) Otherwise, my experience in track and field was in high school as a mediocre sprinter.

So, on a pre-set date, I sat down one evening to smoke, one after the other, every cigarette in my home, in one big, disgusting 'smoke-out'. It was awful, and the taste in my mouth the next morning was (as my father used to say), 'like the whole German army had marched barefoot over my tongue'. Nevertheless, I set out the next morning on my first trial run for distance. Luckily I then lived in Bridge of Allan, Stirlingshire, where the air was clean and the Ochil Hills behind the village were inviting. Conversion was instantaneous.

I went on to do more than 180 races, including five marathons, 45 half-marathons and many shorter races, mostly 10 km. (26) I quit the longer distances only because of knee issues that came inevitably with ageing, but until age 71, I still could run 10 km in fewer minutes than my age in years. If this sounds boastful, then so be it!

26 26.2 MILES, OR 42 KILOMETRES

Distance running began for me as a way to replace one addiction, smoking, with another (see 25). One thing led to another, so I've done races over distances ranging from 1.7 to 26.2 miles, from 1985 to 2020. The latter distance is a marathon, of which I did five, from 1987-1991. These experiences yielded some of the biggest thrills of my life.

The first marathon was in Glasgow, starting and finishing on Glasgow Green. As a first-timer, I was nervous but had support from my partner and her family, which meant a lot in a debut effort. I recall little about the race, except that onlooking children at the roadside offered me sweeties, which I felt obliged to accept, although this had not been part of my pre-race planning. I also recall having to watch out for runaway wheelchairs, as Glasgow's hills meant that such hazardous surprises could happen. Best of all was passing the 22-mile point, which marks the 'Wall', when circulating glucose is finished and needs to be replaced by stored glycogen. I knew by then that I would finish the race, even if I had to crawl to the finish line. It was absolutely exhilarating.

The second was New York, in 1988. The race covers all the five boroughs, starting on Staten Island, then on to Brooklyn, Queens, the Bronx, and finishing in Manhattan. Except for the bridges, the streets were lined all the way, often many persons deep, giving tremendous support to the thousands of runners. This crowd support occurred in all the neighbourhoods, from the Orthodox Jewish areas of Brooklyn to the African-American parts of the Bronx. Their shouts of encouragement carried you along, part of a river of runners. The finish was in Central Park, which most folks think is flat, but by the end, even its gentle inclines are testing. You turn into the Park just past the Plaza Hotel, but more than one exhausted runner missed the turn and had to be re-directed back.

New York makes a weekend of its marathon. The day before the big race, they hosted the international breakfast run of 10 km, starting at the United Nations Building on the East River and finishing at Tavern on the Green, in Central Park. This was a warm-up fun run, with runners relaxed, some costumed, many just jogging. At the start, we lined up next to the UN's array of national flags, to run at the outset with compatriots, but soon we were all mixed together, in an international *mélange*. I ran at times during the race with Russians, Latin Americans, Asians, etc., all chatting away. But this race also brought out eccentricities. I ran by one man with a sign on this back saying that he would play the clarinet as he ran, from start to finish. He was playing 'When the Saints Go Marching In', over and over again. Another man was painting a picture as he ran, having started with a blank canvas. He held it in his left hand, and there was a row of small paint pots along the base, and he painted with his right hand, never breaking stride. When we got to the Tavern, there were hot drinks and juice, and fruit and bagels waiting. Wonderful!

Third came Berlin, in 1989, and my best performance at 3 hours 36 minutes, which was still far behind your typical running addict. Like New York, it had a pre-race warm-up 10 kilometre run, which finished in the old stadium where Hitler's hubris had been foiled by Jesse Owens' sprinting prowess in the 1932 Olympics. For us, it was the venue for a big pasta party for those who wanted to load up on carbs.

The race occurred just months before the Wall was to fall, and tension was already in the air. As we runners assembled in the park near the Reichstag, some began to drift over to the Wall, and a few brave ones decided to do their pre-race stretching exercises *against* it, watched by armed East German border guards above. The trickle became a flow, which I joined. No harm came of it, perhaps a prelude to what was coming later that year, when it was breached. The race itself was on a course as flat as a pancake but covered only West

Berlin. The following year, post-Wall, the course was changed to include East Berlin as well. We ran past notable sights, such as Checkpoint Charlie, to finish in the 'Ku-dam', the main shopping street of the city. Notable was the presence of musical groups on elevated stages along the route; my favourite was the Brazilian samba band, perhaps helping me to my personal best time.

Fourth was London, in 1990, then vying with New York to be the world's biggest marathon, with about 26,000 runners. Like New York, there were multiple starting points, as a single start would be too congested. Even then, for slowpokes like me at the back, it took more than 10 minutes just to get to the starting line. The start was in Greenwich and the finish on Westminster Bridge by the Houses of Parliament. In between we ran past London's sites, such as the Tower of London, The Mall, Buckingham Palace, etc. But it was not all easy going. Part of the route was in Dockland, then undeveloped and devoid of spectators, so it made for a few miles of lonely running. Other sections were on cobblestones, which was hard on the soles. Support was greatest on The Mall, with huge crowds.

Fifth, and last, was Dublin. My friend, Ken Logue, came with me for support and we had good times drinking Guinness in that lovely city. Perhaps that's why the race never really came off for me. I had not trained enough, and the field of runners was small and quiet compared to the bigger marathons. I struggled, even had to walk a bit on the uphills, and thought about packing it in. I have never failed to finish a race but have been tempted to do so a few times!

My racing tailed off after the Millennium, although I still ran the scenic Coniston 14 (miles) in England's Lake District in 2005, aged 60. The distances declined with my ageing knees to only 5 or 10 km races, and some years were even race-less. Heart disease took its toll, but after major open heart surgery (bypasses, valve replacement, etc.) in October, 2018, things improved. (see **40**) Seven months later, I ran the Oxford Town and Gown 10km race, with the Merton College team. Triumphant comeback, but my pace and time were plodding. Even so, after Covid runs its course, I'll be putting on my racing shoes again!

27 BECOMING SCOTTISH

I was born in the USA but moved to the UK in 1965. I went to the UK to do postgraduate study but then stayed on. Eventually it seemed apt to become naturalised as a British citizen. I'd have preferred it to be Scottish citizenship, but that was not an option, as Scotland remains part of the UK (at least as I write). As I recall, my main reason for seeking the change was to be able to vote in Scottish elections.

To be frank, I can't remember how the process began, but it involved form-filling and soliciting references. Looking back, I see now that it was astonishingly easy and straightforward compared with the complex and expensive procedure today. A single hitch emerged: The necessary criteria included a lengthy period of unbroken residence in the UK. I can't recall the exact length of this period, but it was not unreasonable, at least for most persons who would be willing to skip a year's annual holiday abroad.

So, what was the problem? My research was on wild chimpanzees, which meant regular field trips to Africa. My academic career depended on this, as well as trips to international conferences to report the results of this research. Every time I went abroad, the residence 'clock' reverted to zero, and it was clear that I could not do my job *and* fulfil the requirements for naturalisation. My boss at the university, Prof. Peter McEwen, was sympathetic and wrote what seemed like a reasonable and convincing appeal letter to the Home Office, but they rejected it.

I was about to give up, when someone suggested the standard solution for getting something governmental done: Write to your MP. But why would Dennis Canavan, the sitting Member of Parliament for Stirlingshire and Clackmannanshire, take time to assist someone who'd never been able to vote? Perhaps to gain a single vote in future? I had nothing to lose and the strategy worked. He intervened and I was granted citizenship. Needless to say, I voted for him in every election until he retired!

There remained the status of my American citizenship, for at that time, Americans were not allowed to have dual citizenship. So, I went along to the USA Consulate in Edinburgh to renounce my birthright. When I told the clerk at the desk of my intentions, he was clearly perturbed. He said he'd not had such a case before, and he must get his supervisor. The supervisor appeared and advised me of the seriousness of my proposed change, emphasising that this was an irreversible step. I assured him of my intentions and signed the forms, but I think he went away shaking his head.

28 COACHING

I played basketball for long past my sell-by date, through junior high, high school and college in Oklahoma, then in graduate school in Oxford and post-grad studies in Edinburgh (see **22**). I even played after I became a lecturer at Stirling University, but eventually I gave up the sport, or so I thought.

Then the captain of the Stirling University Ladies Basketball Club approached me about coaching them. She was one of my psychology students and a good one, so I paid attention. SULBC was the doormat of the Scottish Universities league, which was perennially dominated by Edinburgh University. I had never coached before, so the prospects seemed dim. But it was a new challenge that would keep me in touch with the hoops game, so I said yes.

I realised that a particular strategy dating back to my school years was not being used by any of the teams in the league. It was a form of zone defence that can quickly turn into a fast-break attack, when possession of the ball is gained. Luckily, the girls provided the potential talent to make the strategy work, although it meant teaching the system to them from scratch. I likened each position to an animal with attributes necessary to play it well. At the point of the 1-3-1 defence was a 'Terrier', a tiny Malaysian girl who harried the opposition's point guard into mistakes. She was backed up by the 'Stork', in the midst of the three, a Scottish girl whose height and long reach was needed to keep the opposition from penetrating our centre. The two wings were the 'Hawks' (one Scottish, one English), quick to pounce and streak down court for quick and easy baskets. Key to it all was the 'Panther', the Scottish captain who'd recruited me, who had to move quickly and effortlessly from side to side along the back line, overseeing the whole and seeking to pin an opposition player in the corner.

It took a while to get the system working smoothly, but when it did, it began to pay off. We started winning matches, and the student newspaper began to report results. That meant that fellow students begin to come along to watch the girls play. Before then, we'd often played with no spectators at all, except the odd boyfriend or two.

The turning point came on a road trip to Aberdeen, our furthest-away match. It had to be done in one day, up and back, and I drove the minibus (of course). The girls overcame a good Aberdeen team to pull off an impressive road victory. After that, we never looked back.

Eventually the season came down to a final match at home against Edinburgh. By then, we had a raucous supportive crowd, who were up for an upset and winning the championship. The girls played their hearts out, but we lost, and so had to be satisfied with finishing second in the league. But a strong statement was made, the captain won the first colours for ladies' basketball in the university's history, and there was next season to look forward to.

Except, not for me. The club decided to get a proper coach for the next season, and I was dumped. They went on to win the championship, beating Edinburgh along the way.

29 WEST HIGHLAND WAY

Throughout my life, from Boy Scouts onwards, I've done my share of hiking in rural or wilderness areas, on five continents. Chasing chimpanzees over 40 years entailed many days spent walking, sometimes in rough terrain, such as the Mahale Mountains of Tanzania or the Nimba Mountains of Guinea. Nothing matched up to the West Highland Way.

This venerable long-distance trail stretches 96 miles (154 km), from Milngavie (a suburb of Glasgow) to Fort William, over a varied range of landscapes in western Scotland. Most walkers do it from south to north, because the challenges of the route increase as one advances northward. Three of us, my girlfriend, her uncle and I, set out with back-packs from Milngavie on a July day, dropped off at the start by her aunt. Each of us had a rucksack with clothing (including rain gear), sleeping bag and mat, and personal items. We also carried split between us a camping stove and minimal cooking gear, water bottles and mess kit, and some food, but not a tent. Instead of tenting, we planned to sleep in a variety of shelters along the way, testing each of five types for at least one night. Bed-and-breakfast accommodation and small hotels were familiar enough, but we also sampled youth hostel, bunkhouse and bothy.

Perhaps the latter three types need some description. Hostels were no longer just for young people, as the modern version catered for people of all ages, including families. Toilets and showers were shared facilities, but divided by sex, as were sleeping arrangements. Most meals were self-catered, but bedding was supplied. Bunkhouses were similar but more sparsely appointed. Rooms were small and fitted with bunkbeds, but guests supplied their own bedding. We three were lucky to get a room for four to ourselves. All meals were self-catered, and provision of food to purchase was limited. The bothy was the most spartan of the five, typically being an unattended, weatherproof, single-roomed hut with almost no furniture, no electricity or running water, but an open fireplace. Users were expected to cater entirely for themselves, and if they used firewood, to add or leave enough for the next folk who came along. There was no system of booking, so you never knew upon turning up whether it would be occupied or empty. If the former, you were expected to make do, as best you could.

We decided to do the walk in eight days, so roughly 12 miles per day. Some folks do it slower, some faster. There is even a long-distance race over the same route, in which runners do the whole length in less than two days, stopping only to eat and drink en route. Our first day was a breeze, getting settled into our stride and pace, taking us to a bed-and-breakfast in Drymen (12 miles). Easy peasy. The second day took us to the shores of Scotland's most iconic lake, Loch Lomond, and on the way, we got our first taste of altitude, over the Conic Hill, finishing at the hostel at Rowardennan (15 miles). A bit more challenging. The third day's route followed the eastern shore of Loch Lomond, with a stop for lunch at Inversnaid, finishing at Inverarnan. Pleasant and easy enough, but any stop for a break at lochside meant testing encounters with midges (14 miles). The fourth day, away from the loch, meant more challenging terrain and some rain, so we finished outside Tyndrum, where early the next morning, we cooked breakfast on the covered platform of the empty railway station (12 miles).

Day 5 took us into more remote Highland areas, with no more shops for the next three days. With the first Munros on the route looming (**51**), we met real inclines with ups and downs that took us in the rain to a bothy in the middle of nowhere (9 miles). Day 6 was the toughest of all, as the route crossed the wild and windswept Rannoch Moor, in constant rain. It was a joy to reach the shelter of Kings House Hotel, overlooked by the towering slopes of the imperious Buachaille. Its photo is to be found on every calendar depicting Scottish wilderness sites. (10 miles) Really challenging. The seventh day took us up Glen Coe, then the route cut away up and over the steepest slopes yet, on the aptly-named Devil's Staircase, to finish at the bunkhouse at Kinlochleven (9 miles). Shortest day yet but most tiring. Of the last day, I have few clear memories, except passing more Munros and walking through forest, finishing at last at Fort William (15 miles). It felt strange to be walking city streets again, even after only a week. We caught the bus back to Glasgow, subdued and tired, but triumphant.

Now, decades later, I'm thinking of doing it again…

30 SUPER BOWL SURPRISE

In 1990, I had my one and only chance to see first-hand an NFL Super Bowl, when the San Francisco 49ers played the Denver Broncos in the Superdome in New Orleans. My hosts in the 'Big Easy' were Don and Elizabeth. She and I had collaborated on primatological research, but I knew him less well.

On the evening before the game, we decided to have pizza, and Don and I went in his car to pick up the takeaway meal. Upon returning to their stately home in the upscale St. Charles Avenue district of the city, Don parked the car outside their house. At this point, a car pulled up behind us, and four African-Americans with handguns piled out and surrounded our car. It was a hold-up. Don said nothing but just reached for his wallet, then got out of the car on his (driver's) side. I sat there, stunned, but started to follow suit. Then things happened very quickly. Don tossed his wallet to the nearest robber, then sprinted for the garage. At the same time, two gunshots were fired. By the time I got out of the car, the four assailants were running back to their car, to make their getaway.

Don returned to the car. We both were shaken but guessed that the shots had been fired in the air, to frighten us. Then we saw a bullet hole in his side of the car. I don't know where the second shot went. He never explained why he had run to the garage, but I imagined that he was trying to convince them that he was going to get his own firearm. (He was an ex-Marine who had seen combat in Vietnam.)

We rang the police, who came quickly. As we described the events to them, they said that they recognised the gang by their *modus operandi*. Apparently they had been doing these hit-and-run robberies for a few days and had killed at least one of their victims. So, I guess we got off lightly!

The 49ers, led by Joe Montana, easily won the football game (55-10), but I recall less about it than about the night before.

31 INCARCERATION

My Uncle Mike, who was a US Deputy Marshall, sometimes suggested locking me in a jail cell, on the grounds that this would be a learning experience of use to any young man. (For some reason, females were not mentioned.) He never acted on this, and I learned to ignore it, as a joke.

Once I did spend some time in a jail cell. I was invited to a conference on chimpanzee conservation, to be held in the Abidjan, Ivory Coast. The organisers in their advance information said that EU citizens did not require a visa, although others did. Accordingly, I booked and flew via Paris on Air France, only to be detained at the airport for attempted illegal entry into the country. It turned out that I should have got a visa before leaving. I was put in a holding cell and told that I would be sent home on the next AF flight, back to Paris.

This development astonished me, and I thought that there must be some misunderstanding. I was perplexed as to what to do, as I'd been offered no chance to be in touch with anyone, for example, the British Embassy.

Meanwhile, local occupants of the cell opposite to me gestured that I should offer the jailer a bribe. I shook my head in refusal, but as the hours wore on, I wavered. I tried to engage the jailer in conversation, with my limited French and his limited English, attempting to convey this intention without blatantly incriminating myself. He eventually became very gruff and told me to shut up.

Luckily, before I gave in to complete despair, someone from the conference showed up and sprung me. Apparently, other British delegates had had similar experiences earlier in the day, so the organisers were alerted to come for me, after my non-appearance at the conference hotel.

I was never able to tell my uncle about this sobering experience, but I'm sure that he would have sagely nodded his head.

32 DEER ME!

One winter during my sojourn in Ohio, we drove into town for an evening at a friend's house. Visiting us at the time was Linda's mother, from Jersey City. As we drove in, the roadside was clear, but on the way home a couple of hours later, it was not. Hence begins the story.

On the roadside was the victim of a deer strike, an adult white-tailed deer doe, dead from being hit by a vehicle. Given that this had to be a fresh kill, it seemed a good idea to scavenge the carcass for venison, so I stopped the car and humped the carcass into the car's boot. Linda's mother seemed bemused by this, though I could not see why. Probably uncommon behaviour in Jersey City.

My plan was to leave it overnight, as the temperature was already below freezing, then gut it in the morning. Then, I would obtain a deer 'tag', as required by Ohio state law, and take it to a specialist butcher who did wild game. I imagined a freezer full of steaks and joints, maybe even some sausages.

However, when I opened the boot the next day, it became clear that I'd made a big mistake. I had not taken into account elementary thermal dynamics. Although the ambient temperature was below freezing, the core temperature of the carcass had not dropped nearly low enough overnight. The doe was now swollen and smelly. The good luck had turned bad.

Now I had to get rid of the stinking carcass. I could not take it back to the kill site, in broad daylight, and risking someone calling the authorities. I could not bury it on our property, as the ground was frozen solid. All I could think to do was to drag it into the woods, far enough away from the house to avoid the stench and leave it for the coyotes. I dragged it down to the bottom of the nearby ravine, but when I looked up, I realised that our neighbour's house was just above. I could not ditch the problem on them, so I dragged it a further 100 metres, only to have to repeat the procedure. Eventually, I dragged it several hundred metres, outside the Springwood housing development, after much effort, and abandoned it.

In the end, the only beneficiaries of my impulsive scavenging were the coyotes. Lesson learned (see **93**).

33 INVESTMENTS GONE AWRY

As the son of an accountant, I should be savvy about what to do with money. Sadly, not always so, as instanced by my foray into horse racing (see **34**). Here are two other examples:

While living in Ohio, I grew fond of the beers produced by a regional micro-brewery, Oldenberg. Every one of their beers that I tried tasted great. So, when a chance to invest in ownership came up, I bought 200 shares in the company. At first, it was good fun. The annual meetings at the brewery were convivial and informative. Success and ambitious expansion brought concerns, such as opening brew-pubs in university towns, which we thought to be a sure-fire way to grow and prosper. It turned out that most college students don't have the money or taste to appreciate high-quality craft beers. We could not compete with the Bud Lites of the world. So, our over-extension led to bankruptcy.

Another scheme came from my erstwhile field assistant in Tanzania, Moshe Bunengwa. We had formed a friendship based on shared hours of chasing chimpanzees in the Mahale Mountains. Later, he wrote to me with a plan to make us both rich. He proposed to row across Lake Tanganyika at night to what was then Zaire (now DRC). There he would meet surreptitiously with miners who would smuggle gold out of the mines and sell it to him for hard currency. Then he would take the gold to Tanzania's biggest city, Dar es Salaam, and sell it, equally discreetly, to Arab merchants, who were uneasy about their shaky situation in Tanzanian society. In order to build up a nest-egg, they would pay much more for the gold than he had paid to the Zairean miners. Everyone would be happy with this win-win situation, and we would profit. Pure basic capitalism.

All Moshe needed was cash dollars to start the process going, so I sent some to him. Gullible as I am, I'm not sure that I *really* believed in this scheme, but I was so impressed by his entrepreneurial spirit that I could not let him down. As you may have guessed, no rich profits emerged, but later I heard from friends at Mahale that my field assistant had secured another young wife...

34 HORSES FOR COURSES

When I first spent time in Cambridge, in 2003, it was important to find a 'local', that is a favoured pub in the neighbourhood, to patronise regularly. After auditioning them all, I chose The Free Press, because it was small, friendly, non-smoking, and offered a good selection of real ales. Fair enough, nothing unusual about that.

The publican, Craig Bickley, was an ex-jockey, and after due diligence, he made an unexpected and enterprising proposal to the regulars at the pub: we should form a syndicate and buy a racehorse! I had no knowledge whatsoever of horse racing, but along with 10 others, I signed up. Craig's proposal was simple: each of us was to pay in a certain amount of money each month, to support first the purchase, then housing and training of the horse. We would make use of his contacts in the racing world to do this, and then we would be off and running, so to speak.

We bought a young filly and installed her with a trainer at Epsom. They would bring her up to speed and enter her in races that suited her characteristics and fitness. She was registered as FreePressionist, and we chose our silks, after much lubricated discussion. Both of these aspects required originality, as we could not duplicate any existing predecessors. Our job as owners was just to go along to the races, which could be anywhere in central England, and watch her win fame and fortune. Craig did warn us that the chances of such success were small, that only a few horses actually made enough money from winnings for a surplus to accrue, but that didn't stop us from dreams of The Derby.

So, periodically, we would meet at the pub, pile into vehicles and head for a racecourse. The experience was exciting, with wagering and drinking and badinage. Although our filly occasionally ran well and was even placed a few times, she did not win, and the months went by. Then, one cold evening at Wolverhampton, she did. What jubilation! Photographs with her and the jockey in the winner's circle (Fig. 23). Champagne in the owners' lounge. Most importantly, Craig told us, this ensured her long-term future, for as a winner, she would become a brood mare, rather than dog food.

The syndicate eventually petered out, and we sold her on accordingly. I pass on this important lesson: if you ponder having a go at such an enterprise, be sure to base it in a pub. That way, when you come back from the races, win or lose, there will always be drinks on the house, either in celebration or commiseration!

35 DEADLY HOBBY

It seems that everyone has hobbies, if these are defined as activities done for personal pleasure, with no necessary resulting pay-off to self or society. Thus, hobbies range from train-spotting to blood donation. I have my share of the typical ones: cinema-going, football-watching, vegetable-growing, etc – but the most unusual one for me has been litter-collecting in a cemetery.

The city of Cambridge has three municipal, that is, secular burial grounds, for which it takes responsibility, at least in principle. In practice, like most local authorities, it is budgetarily overstretched, so it does the minimum of maintenance. One of those three was in my neighbourhood of Castle Hill, where a group of locals founded the Friends of Histon Road Cemetery, in order to assist in its upkeep. We had varied tasks voluntarily assigned according to skills and preferences of the members. My job was to pick up litter in the cemetery once a week. Others did more demanding and interesting jobs, such as repair of gravestones or planting and pruning.

Why would a cemetery need such litter collection? Because this cemetery was treated more as a park or playground or dossing spot for street people or a lovers' lane for teenagers. The latter two functions were facilitated by mature shrubbery, creating spots for privacy. The cemetery was never locked, so there was 24/7 access, which is admirable in principle but in practice an invitation for discarding rubbish. So I spent every Sunday morning, early before anyone else was up, doing my rounds with plastic bin bag and heavy gloves. Because of the varied activities, there were more than empty bottles or fast-food containers to be gathered up. I encountered plenty of used syringes, needles and condoms. I never rousted still-sleeping homeless folks, and those that saw me ignored my presence.

So, what beside tidiness made this hobby rewarding? I found many things besides rubbish. Stolen bicycles were fairly common, presumably taken for a joy-ride, then abandoned. I found jewellery a couple of times, and a fine stainless steel wristwatch. Once I found an intact wallet containing Canadian cash to the amount of $90. All of these had to go to the police lost property office, in case owners sought them.

The deal was that if the items were unclaimed after 30 days, then the finder got them. I never went back for the bicycles, but I did for the wallet. Happily for me, it was unclaimed, probably lost by a tourist, long gone. The strangest find was the contents of a woman's purse, with credit cards, etc., strewn about. Strange, because it belonged to another of the members of the Friends, from whom it had been stolen, so I could return it directly to her.

36 NEVER AGAIN!

Some things you need to do only once in your life. Afterwards you're glad you did them, but you'd never do them again. (37) Here are two examples:

White-water canoeing in northern Wisconsin, with a group of old college friends. Two of us in the open aluminium canoe, with me at the front, to fend off rocks that suddenly emerged from the rushing water. The other person, experienced at this activity, in the back to steer. We sat only 10 feet apart, but with the sound of the water, I could rarely make out what he was shouting, so we had many collisions. The water was not deep but it was cold, and we were wet from the outset, from the spray. If that wasn't enough, we capsized twice, which required righting the boat and emptying it of water in order to continue. I swallowed a lot of water but was never in mortal danger. Invigorating but exhausting. We recovered with food and drinks afterward, in front of a rustic open fire.

Ice-climbing in the Scottish Highlands, at Glencoe, in March, with three others. I was roped into this, as a favour to a colleague, Cat Hobaiter, who was hosting a Japanese visitor, Tetsuro Matsuzawa, who was a serious mountaineer, having done major summits in the Himalayas. He and Cat were experienced climbers, but her postgraduate student (similarly 'recruited') and I were neophytes. We were all right until we got to the near-vertical ice face, when we donned crampons and took ice axes in hand. To ascend, you must stab the ice face with your spike-toed crampons, then reach up to stab it with your ice axe, alternately shifting your body-weight from one to the other, alternately. The higher you went, the greater the risk of an injurious fall, if you didn't stab efficiently. We were advised not to look down, just up. It was frightening, but upwards was the easy part. Coming back down meant reversing the process, but you couldn't see when you were descending the ice face, so you had to keep looking around and down, forced to confront the daunting task. It all worked out fine, safely down, but it was a relief to be back on bare rock again. Glasses were raised later in the evening.

37 ETHEREAL DIVING

When an academic retires, there is usually a celebratory meal and a gift given by students and colleagues. The latter is sometimes an antiquarian book, such as a first edition of one of Darwin's (dream on!), a fine old print, or a bottle of fine whisky or brandy. In my case, in 2011, at 67 years old, the gift was merely an envelope, and I recall thinking, "Surely they could have done better than just a card." The envelope contained more than a card, for it also had an invitation and a voucher for a sky-dive. With all eyes on me, waiting for a response, all I could say was, "This certainly is a surprise." Such a response was hardly original and surely an understatement, as the topic had never been mentioned. All I could do was grin and bear it.

An excursion was organised to an airfield near Cambridge, and we had a jolly anticipatory picnic. Then the time came to do the deed, so the student who'd master-minded the event, Maura Reilly, and I adjourned to the briefing. She was an experienced sky-diver, but I was a complete novice. To give a flavour of the briefing, we were told how to avoid breaking a leg upon landing, the most dangerous part of the jump. Maura could second that, as she admitted that she had done just that on her first dive! Not reassuring.

We were told not to fear the impact when we hit the ground, which would be no worse than you got from jumping off a 10-foot-high wall. I thought to myself, "I've never jumped off such a wall and it sounds a bit dicey." Of course, I just nodded.

Before we knew it, the group of divers, including Maura as my minder, were airborne, headed for 10-11,000 feet altitude, for the drop. We sat on the floor of the plane, queued up and ready to take our turn to defenestrate via the open doorway. The moment of truth came when it was your turn, sitting there, legs dangling out the side of the plane. You look down to the ground *so far* below, with nothing between you and it but air. There's little to do at that point except to launch yourself out.

A sky-dive comes in two stages: free-fall and parachute. Free-fall was fast, noisy, rushing air and staying right-side-up, with little time to really notice anything. When the parachute opened, there was total silence and the feeling of being as light as a feather. Time to look around and enjoy the experience, like a soaring bird. After some time (who knows how long?), the ground starts getting notably closer, and you remember to take a sitting position with your legs fully extended in front of you. Before you know it, you're back on grassy *terra firma*, landing with a slight bump on your bottom, not your feet. Then, you're standing up, unhitching the gear, totally flushed with adrenalin. Wow!

38 TRAVELS

Field primatologists generally have to choose between Africa, Asia, or South America when focusing on their subjects, as that is where you will find the primates. I chose Africa, which explains the predominance of those countries on this list. Scientific conferences take academicians to all sorts of places, which accounts for many of the European countries, as do holidays. There are visits and there are visits, so here a 4-star system makes clear how long such visits were: Blank = less than a week; * = more than a week; ** = more than a month; *** = more than a year; **** = more than a decade. (Stars are based on total time, over multiple visits.)

Algeria

Argentina

Austria*

Bahamas

Belgium

Brazil*

Burkina Faso

Burundi

Canada*
Canary Islands*
Chile
Congo (Dem. Repub.)**
Costa Rica*
Denmark
England****
France**
Gabon**
Gambia*
Germany (E & W)***
Gibraltar
Guinea (Repub.)*
Hungary**
India*
Indonesia*
Ireland (Repub.)**
Israel*
Italy**
Ivory Coast
Jamaica*
Japan**
Jersey
Kenya**
Mali
Malaysia

Mexico**
Morocco
Netherlands
Niger
Nigeria
Northern Ireland (Ulster)
Poland
Portugal*
Puerto Rico**
Romania*
Russia*
Rwanda
Scotland****
Senegal***
Singapore
Slovenia
South Africa*
Spain**
Switzerland*
Tanzania***
Thailand
Tunisia*
Turks and Caicos*
Uganda**
USA****
Wales

Some strictly personal preferences. Countries of the 60 listed, not to be revisited: Russia, Democratic Republic of Congo.

Countries to be revisited (plus 4-star ones): Germany, Ireland, Senegal. Countries unlikely to be visited: China, Middle East. Countries not visited, but on my bucket list: Czech Republic, Greece, Ethiopia, Namibia.

39 FLASH-BULB MEMORIES

Psychologists have a name for a particular kind of episodic memory when an event has such a powerful, sometimes shocking effect that its context is forever fixed. That is, a person recalls where and when, as well as what they were doing, when they heard the news. Such 'flash-bulb' memories seem to be universally human, and sometimes may affect millions at one time. My parents' generation had such a memory of 7 December, 1941, the date of the Japanese attack on Pearl Harbor, Hawaii. Current generations have much the same traumatic memory about 11 September, 2001, when the Twin Towers in New York City and the Pentagon in Washington, DC were attacked ('9/11'). I suspect that many folks also will have one for 6 January, 2021, when Trumpian crowds stormed and briefly occupied the Capitol Building of the USA government.

My first such memory is of 23 November 1963, when President John F Kennedy was assassinated in Dallas, Texas, while riding in an open-topped car, in a motorcade through the city's centre. Ironically, I learned of it from someone's transistor radio while at a shooting range, target shooting with a rifle, as a required part of ROTC training (see **4**). I was an undergraduate student at the University of Oklahoma. We abandoned the class and rushed off to find a television.

My next one also was an assassination, of Robert Kennedy, killed on 6 June 1968, just after an election rally in Los Angeles. He was killed by a lone gunman while campaigning for president. I learned of it in Oxford, England, walking to lunch in college, past the Bodleian Library, when I heard a newspaper-seller shouting the news as he sold copies of the *Oxford Mail*.

Next came John Lennon's death, on 8 December 1980, in New York, when he and his wife, Yoko Ono, returned home to their apartment in the Dakota Building in Manhattan. The lone gunman was waiting for them, and Lennon died on the spot. I learned of this while driving home from a day out with my girlfriend on the Blue Ridge Parkway, in western North Carolina. Hearing the news from a car radio, while driving in the dark, somehow enhanced the effect.

On 31 August 1997, I heard of the death of Princess Diana, in a car-crash in Paris, while she and her boyfriend were fleeing from paparazzi photographers. I learned of it on a Sunday morning, while relaxing and reading the Sunday newspapers, at home in Oxford, Ohio.

The sample above suggests that all flash-bulb memories are negative, usually triggered by death. Why are similar effects so rarely stimulated by positive events? Here are two: On 20 July 1969, we stayed up late at night in our flat in Portobello, Scotland, to watch the Apollo 11 mission make the first manned landing on the moon. Neil Armstrong, the first person to step on the moon's surface, uttered the memorable words "One small step for a man, one giant step for mankind." This was not a shocking event but a much-anticipated one, with a happy ending. Similarly, but perhaps of less global significance, was hearing the news that England had won its first (and so far only) World Cup football championship, on 30 July 1966, as we did basketball training in Tel Aviv (see **21**).

40 HEARTY SEND-OFF

In October 2018, I was found to need major open heart surgery, that is, bypasses, valve replacement, etc.(**26**) As I was to be operated on first thing in the morning, they had me admitted to the Royal Edinburgh Hospital the evening before. At bedtime, a nurse came round and offered to give me something to make me sleep better. She said that a person is understandably nervous the night before a big operation, so such medication would be helpful. I agreed, thinking that she'd come back with a glass of water and a couple of pills. Then she asked, "Would you prefer sherry or whisky?" She must have seen the confusion in my face, as I tried to divine if she was joking or not. She then said (perhaps a bit defensively?) it was medicinal and only 25 ml. I asked for a wee dram of the latter and slept soundly.

ACADEMIA

41 PUBLISH OR PERISH

Be forewarned, reader! This vignette may be the most didactic and empirical of the lot. It may tax your patience, but not so much as if I pressed upon you my single-spaced, 31-page *curriculum vitae!*

Academic careers are judged by their productivity, which basically means their publications. The catch-phrase 'Publish or perish' is no joke. Hiring, tenure, promotion, etc. in academia all ultimately depend on putting knowledge into the public domain, so the products of scholarly labour are published books, chapters or journal articles. This enterprise may sound straightforward, but it entails much more than just generating publications, as will be seen below.

Here are my basic statistics: Over a career spanning 1963-2020 (so, 57 years), 477 academic products of my scholarly industry so far have been published. These include 8 books, 56 book chapters in edited volumes, and 175 articles in scientific periodicals. This output is hardly a stunning number, averaging only about eight publications per year. The articles range from a few paragraphs to 53 pages and show the most variable content. Each of these categories deserves more explanation.

Books. Three of my books are single authored, one is jointly authored, and four are jointly edited. This order reflects the relative scholarly prestige of each category, so single authored is best. Six of the eight were published by university presses, the sort of publishers that most lay readers are unlikely to encounter in everyday life. Edited volumes result when a few academics combine efforts to edit (compile) a book consisting of invited chapters by a set of authors expert in a topic.

Chapters. These are the contributions that make up such an edited volume, which succeeds or not based on the skill of the editors in selecting an arresting topic and assembling a compelling line-up of commissioned contributors to present their best work. University presses are preferred, and these often reflect the relative status of their host institutions, such as Cambridge, Harvard, Oxford, Yale, etc.

Articles. These publications vary so much that I divide them into two sub-categories: Journal Articles (175), and Notes, Reviews, Comments, Letters, Translations, Popular Articles, and Other Trivia (238). Most of the articles were in peer-reviewed scientific journals; of the latter, the vast majority were book reviews. Labelling these as trivia is a bit misleading, as sometimes a brief published comment has more impact that a longer, unstimulating article.

'Peer review' means that publication depends on satisfying the editor(s), and at least two reviewers who have scrutinised and critiqued the manuscript, that it meets exacting scientific standards. Thus, it is a meritocratic form of quality control. So is academic success just a matter of adding up the numbers? Not by a long shot! Anyone can self-publish a book if they are willing to pay all the publishing costs. Similarly, there are many scientific journals that require the authors to pay for publication, thus the phrase 'pay to play'. I have not made use of this latter avenue to publication, so cannot say more about it.

Productivity is measured not by *quantity* of publications

but by their *quality*. How to judge quality? One way is by *citations*, that is, the number of times that an author's publication is then cited (referred to) in other publications. All other things being equal, the amount of attention that a paper gets is a measure of its impact. Most products of academic endeavour are never cited at all. Harsh reality! That applies to most of my trivia; after all, who needs to cite a book review? Most of my 26,000+ citations accrued to this point are to journal articles, books and book chapters.

So, is measuring quality this simple? No. If the articles in the highest quality journals get the most citations, then ambitious academics should strive to publish in them. Every scientist knows that a paper in *Nature* or *Science* means *much* more than if it were published in some less prestigious journal. Thus, an academic can benefit from the *Impact Factor* (IF) of the journal, which is calculated on how often its articles get cited. It all sounds a bit circular, right?

Furthermore, citations can be used to calculate the relative status of an individual author, via a statistic called the *H index,* which is based on how many of their articles have the same number of citations. Thus, if a person has published at least 10 articles, each of which has been cited at least 10 times, they have an *H* index of 10; if it is 20 and 20, then 20; and so on. This is an ever more challenging measure, as *H* rises cumulatively and shows the overall impact of an author over a career. As I write, my *H* index is 81, according to Google Scholar.

By now, the astute reader may suspect that the system

can be gamed. Self-citation, in which an author cites their previous work in their other publications, clearly inflates their citation numbers. Reputable *H* indices exclude these. What about papers with multiple authors, how are they credited? By convention, each author gets the same credit, so that if an article has 10 authors, all 10 get equal benefit. This invites reciprocal citation, that is, if you cite me in yours, then I'll cite you, or include you as a co-author on mine. And so on. Of my non-trivial publications, only a quarter are single-authored. In primatology, especially field work, collaboration, and so co-authorship, is rightly the norm.

Multi-authored publications may have scores of authors in some fields (such as genetics), so how is the reader to know which author(s) actually made the key contributions? Traditionally, the first author listed (usually the 'corresponding author') is accorded the most credit. Of my articles and chapters, I was first-author on 47%. And, so it goes...

Perhaps the reader has seen enough to realise that in the ivory tower of academia, there is no easy way to gauge quality, that academicians are no less competitive than those in other professions, and that there are empirical ways to make judgements, although none is perfect.

42 DEGREES OF DIFFICULTY

An academician needs degrees, in order to operate. I ended up with a surfeit, *but* two of them are somewhat questionable...

My undergraduate degree was Bachelor of Science, majoring in zoology, with minors in history and mathematics (1965). This was done in three years at the University of

Oklahoma, in Norman, my childhood home town. I had superb mentors, Profs. Charles Carpenter (herpetology) and Cluff Hopla (entomology), both accomplished naturalists. (43)

My first postgraduate degree was a Doctor of Philosophy from the University of Oxford (1970). (Typical of Oxford's exceptionalism, its doctorates aren't PhDs like almost everywhere else, but are DPhils.) I started there in zoology but switched to experimental psychology (although I rarely did an experiment). It took three different research projects before I finally finished, with an observational study of pre-school-aged children, which was published as my first book. My final mentor, Prof. David Vowles, was an ethological physiologist who studied ring doves.

Twenty years later (1990), I took a second doctorate, a PhD in social anthropology from the University of Stirling. My supervisor, Dr Alison Bowes, sent me back to the classroom for the basics. Attending lectures with students less than half my age was a timely, even humbling experience, for someone in mid-career. I did the degree in order to switch from psychology to anthropology, realising that to make such a change meant getting new qualifications.

At that point, enough seemed enough, but...

Shortly before he left Corpus Christi College, Cambridge, the *praelector*, Berthold Kress, asked me if I would like to have a Cambridge PhD by incorporation. He said he'd never got the chance to do this particular ceremony (like the others, it required of him Latin speeches), and this might be his last opportunity. Astonishingly, all that it entailed was filling in some forms. No fees, no examination. It seems that three universities in the British Isles, that is, Cambridge, Oxford, and Trinity College Dublin, have a reciprocal agreement that anyone who takes a doctorate from one of the three, and then goes to permanent employment at either of the others, can be granted another PhD by the latter, for doing nothing. A complete swizz. So, I said yes. Why not?

On graduation day (2009), I filed down Kings Parade with all the other Corpus graduands, feeling a bit like a charlatan. The ceremony went off without a hitch, but afterwards when I checked the diploma in my hands, it turned out to be for the wrong degree. Instead of a PhD, they'd given me a Master of Arts. Next day, I told Berthold, and he agreed to get it sorted out, and eventually the PhD certificate arrived. But they never asked for the MA one back! So, unexpectedly, I got a 'twofer'.

43 ESTEEMED MENTORS

Behind every successful academician, there has been at least one mentor. This is a truism, but in my chequered career, I was lucky to have had several, listed here in chronological order.

As a teenager, I was helped by **Charles C Carpenter**, known as 'Chuck' to many, but 'Doc' to me. He was a professor of zoology, specialising in behavioural ecology, who focused his career on the Iguanidae, a cosmopolitan family of lizards ranging in size from tiny fence lizards to huge marine iguanas. His positive influence on me went far beyond herpetology. He gave me my first experiences of the field, from the southwestern USA to Mexico (see **9**) to the Bahamas (**12**). He became a lifelong friend.

At the same time, I came under the influence of **Cluff E Hopla**, also a professor of zoology, who specialised in medical entomology. He had influenced me earlier, as a scoutmaster, as his outdoor activities went far beyond the usual weenie roasts and campfires, into natural history. His intrepid ladder-climbing up cliff faces to secure ecto-parasites from the nests of cliff swallows set a standard for doing whatever needed to be done to answer a question. In my many later encounters with insects, such as the termites eaten by chimpanzees, I benefited from his early introduction to entomology.

When I my first doctoral project in zoology ended abruptly, I was an academic orphan, rescued by **John and Corrine Hutt**. In desperation, I approached them 'cold', having never met them, but they generously took me on. John became my supervisor of record, as he had a permanent position at Oxford. Corinne became my actual day-to-day supervisor, facilitating my switch of subjects into human ethology, focusing on pre-school-aged children. She died unexpectedly young, and again I was left academically 'orphaned'.

David M Vowles never meant to be my final mentor at Oxford, for he was a neuro-ethologist specialising in hormonal influences on bird behaviour, in experimental psychology. He saved my bacon when my second doctoral project working with the Hutts was left high and dry. He was frank in saying that he knew little about what I was up to, but he supported me nonetheless, both in finishing the DPhil and as a post-doctoral fellow. The latter came after Oxford, when he got the chair in psychology at the University of Edinburgh and took about half of his team with him. This gave me my first access to Scotland, which was a life-changing move.

David A Hamburg played a crucial part in my transfer to primatology, in several ways. We met by chance, after he gave a lecture at Edinburgh, and I was delegated to drive him to the airport for departure. His flight was delayed, so we had a long, spontaneous talk that led to his offering me a post-doctoral position at Stanford. That job took me first to Delta and then to Gombe, on the lifelong trail of chimpanzees. He was a soft-spoken man who was an excellent listener, but when strong action was needed, he showed it, for example, in sorting out the Gombe kidnapping in 1975.

Alison Bowes never imagined that she would mentor me, but her influence was absolutely crucial. At Stirling, she was senior lecturer in social anthropology, the only anthropologist on staff, whose research had been on Israeli *kibbutzim*. I was a reader in psychology, totally untutored in anthropology. I needed a new qualification, to be gained while being a full-time faculty member at Stirling, so I approached her about supervising my second PhD. Despite my being older than her, and of higher academic rank, and her not being a primatologist, she gave each chapter critical scrutiny. The published version of the PhD later became my most-cited book, thanks largely to her patience and generosity.

None of these mentors gained much from their investment of time and effort into my career, but their example caused me to vow to pass on mentoring like theirs to my students. The most challenging of these was the only one who did not study primates, Helen Newing. Instead, for her PhD she chose to study duikers (forest antelopes) and did a superb job, despite my ignorance of ungulates.

44 CHIMPANZEE DENTISTRY

Although booked to go to Gombe to study wild chimpanzees, Caroline Tutin and I were delayed by Tanzanian bureaucracy beyond our control. Our boss, Prof. David Hamburg, of Stanford University, suggested that while awaiting clearance, we should gain experience of chimpanzees at the Delta Primate Center, in Louisiana. There we found a group of seven wild-born chimpanzees, left behind by the researcher who had previously studied them, Emil Menzel. The apes lived in a 1.5-acre enclosure in the pine woods, cared for by their long-time companion, Palmer ('Pal') Midgett.

We arrived in January 1972, naïve but keen, and Pal showed us the ropes. We decided to spend our time doing ethological studies of their spontaneous behaviour in daily life. Prof. Hamburg had given us free range to study whatever we chose but hoped that something scientifically publishable would result.

Like all normal chimpanzees, they engaged in social and self-grooming on a daily basis. Usually this behaviour was directed to the body surface, especially the hairy parts, in order to remove ecto-parasites, dirt, detritus, body fluids, etc. This activity occupies a surprising proportion of their waking hours, much more than required for hygiene. Instead, grooming seems to be a preferred leisure 'chore', pleasurable in its own right.

Imagine our surprise when one day an adolescent female, Belle, began to groom *inside the mouth* of one of the others. The recipient reclined passively, mouth wide open, while she gave him dental cleaning. Even more impressive was her use of simple wooden probes, made from fragments of tree branches, to aid her efforts. Chimpanzees are renowned makers and users of tools, but mostly for extractive foraging, such as termite-fishing, nut-cracking, etc, but elementary technology for oral hygiene was unknown.

What came next was jaw-dropping (!): Belle started *extracting* teeth. She was doing dentistry! This development confounded us, until we paid closer attention and saw the chimpanzees repeatedly manipulating their own teeth, which were loose. It turned out that they were at the stage of life to be shedding their 'milk' teeth, and Belle was assisting in the process. Later we watched another of the chimpanzees, Bandit, use another type of tool to remove his own loose molar. He looped a ribbon-like strip of cloth around the tooth and used it in a repetitive, dental-flossing motion to dislodge it. The apes were just helping the natural process along.

So the chimpanzees gave us the data for our first scientific article, on a platter! We wrote up a short paper, submitted it to *Nature*, and it was accepted, but this was before the extractions started. When these new developments occurred, we wrote an updated, more popularly-written article for the *Journal of the American Dental Association*, the professional publication read by thousands of dentists. They were happy to take it, with supporting photos for any sceptical readers.

This illustrated account prompted a flood of letters and emails from dentists, who asked for copies of the photos to frame and hang on their waiting room walls. We were happy to oblige but thought that chimpanzees should get benefits from their labours, so we established the Belle Fund to pay for environmental enrichment activities for another group of less-well-off chimpanzees, at the Royal Zoological Society of Scotland (Edinburgh Zoo). We asked the dentists to make donations in any amount, and every single one responded positively. Serendipity for apes and humans alike!

McGrew WC & Tutin CEG (1972) Chimpanzee dentistry. *Journal of the American Dental Association* 85: 1198-1204.

McGrew WC & Tutin CEG (1973) Chimpanzee tool use in dental grooming. *Nature* 241: 477-478.

45 AFTERNOON DELIGHT

At Delta, Caroline Tutin and I were lucky enough to be 'apprenticed' to Palmer Midgett Jr. ('Pal'). We 'inherited' him, along with seven chimpanzees, who occupied an enclosure set amongst loblolly pine forest. Stanford University had bought the chimpanzees upon the retirement of the previous researcher in charge but did not yet have facilities ready for them in California. Our boss there, *in absentia*, was Prof. David Hamburg, then head of Stanford's Human Biology program.

Pal set us to work from the ground up. We learned about cleaning out the apes' night-sleeping quarters and their feeding schedule. They had free indoor-outdoor access 24-7. We took systematic daily records and joined in maintenance of the facilities. Only then did we begin research, that is, to take our own data on chimpanzee behaviour. The enclosure was separate from the main buildings of the Delta Research Center, which focused on laboratory studies of virology. Only gradually did we learn that our semi-isolation afforded a certain flexibility in daily life at the enclosure.

One Friday afternoon, Pal said that it was time to get to know the chimpanzees better, that is, to go into their enclosure *with* them. They were young adults, and one of them, Gigi, gave birth during our time there. We were a bit concerned at this prospect, as chimpanzees are strong and well-dentally-armed creatures, and our experience of visiting the laboratory part of Delta was that the apes there hated humans. Pal said our apes would be okay, as he had known them since their infancy, so we complied.

We donned heavy-duty boiler suits and took some food treats with us into the enclosure. (It must be said that Pal also had put some six-packs of beer in the fridge, so we fortified ourselves in advance. This took TGIF to a new level!). The chimpanzees initially were excited by the newcomers, but we realised quickly that what they wanted was rough-and-tumble play, that is, chasing and wrestling. We tried to persuade them to engage in more sedate activities, such as social grooming, to which some acceded. Pal watched over us, always vigilant and ready to intervene if things started to get out of hand. Thus we spent some happy Friday afternoons, and later when Stanford undergraduates joined us as summer research assistants, they took part too. Now, I shudder to imagine what today's Health and Safety officers would think of this activity.

When the time came for Prof. Hamburg to come for an inspection visit, as his itinerary included a Friday, we pondered what to do. He was, after all, a psychiatrist, not an animal behaviourist, and we had not told him about the extra-curricular activities on Fridays. When we offered him the chance to join in, he immediately agreed, perhaps in some combination of curiosity and novelty-seeking. All went well, but I doubt that he ever mentioned it in his reports to the grant-giving body!

46 APE ESCAPOLOGY

At the Delta Primate Center, the apes' spacious grassy enclosure contained a climbing frame network and other elevated structures. They were confined by a perimeter fence of chain link mesh, topped by inward-sloping smooth aluminium panels. At more than 5 metres height, it was reckoned to be escape-proof, at least in the beginning. However, as the chimpanzees grew in size, strength and experience, they sought to widen their horizons. Emil Menzel, the researcher previously in charge, published two scientific articles on their tool-using escape techniques. They detached sections of the wooden climbing frame, 2" x 4" planks, stood these up against the fence as 'ladders', then ran up them, making a final leap to catch the top of the fence. With even one handhold, a chimpanzee could pull itself up and out of the enclosure. Others followed, sometimes assisting one another.

By the time Caroline Tutin and I arrived, all such boards had been removed, but that did not stop their peregrinations. The apes turned their attention to the poles embedded in the ground, which by repeated rocking back and forth, they loosened from their anchorage. Once uprooted, they dragged the poles to the fence and used them as heavier but equally functional ladders. So, all of these ladder-like objects also had to be removed from the enclosure.

If the reader is wondering why we humans took so long to react, it was because the chimpanzees did not escape to leave but just to have outings. They did so when humans were absent, in early morning or late evening. They returned to the enclosure of their own accord, so that when we arrived in the morning the next day, there were no ladders remaining in place against the fence. Eventually the evidence told against them, as, for example, their raids on the food stores could not be hidden.

Having removed all the pole-ladders, we relaxed, but not for long. The apes still were escaping somehow, but this time we caught them in the act. They used stout sticks fashioned from the foliage that we gave them for nesting as 'pitons'. They climbed the mesh, then thrust the sticks into the thin seams between adjacent panels and used these protrusions as handholds to climb up and out. So, from then on, we had to take more care with their nest materials, to make sure they got twigs and not sticks.

So it went, as a sort of game, with each side seeking to outwit the other. We were forced to appreciate the creative and persistent intelligence of these large-brained cousins of humanity!

McGrew WC, Tutin CEG & Midgett PS (1975) Tool use in a group of captive chimpanzees. I. Escape. *Zeitschrift fuer Tierpsychologie* 37: 146-162

47 THE GREAT ESCAPE

The chimpanzees' rectangular 1.5 acre outdoor enclosure at Delta was an idyllic setting, and the apes were lively and active. They interacted with local wildlife, eating the birds that were foolish enough to venture in and using sticks to chase away snakes.

But problems emerged. The enclosure's design had been escape-proof, even as the chimpanzees grew into adolescence, but by the time we arrived, some had achieved adult size and strength. We knew from Emil Menzel's earlier publications that these clever apes knew how to escape from the enclosure by propping up logs vertically against the fence and using them as ladders to go out over the top, and that they did the same by jamming stick pitons into cracks. After all of these objects had been removed, we relaxed (see **46**).

Research proceeded well, and we were pleased to hear from Stanford that we would get a flying visit from Jane Goodall, who was curious to see what we were doing. This news was thrilling and unexpected, even a little intimidating, as she would be our 'boss' at Gombe. With great pride and pleasure, we took her to the enclosure, where the chimpanzees greeted her with pant hoots and greeting displays, as they did to all strangers. As we walked the periphery of the enclosure, the apes followed along, excited and noisy. But just as we came to the furthest point from the office, on the opposite side, which therefore was the longest distance from the telephone, unexpected developments began.

One of the two adult males began displaying on the mesh, clinging quadrupedally, and his repeated powerful tugging began to pop the metal ties that held the mesh to the frame. One by one, these gave way, peeling the mesh away from the frame and producing an ever-increasing gap in the fence. Very quickly we had an emergency to deal with, and little time to make a plan of response. Caroline set off running back to the office to ring for help, while I stood before the gaping gap in the fence, somehow hoping to persuade them to stay inside (which failed miserably). Soon, the first chimpanzee came out through the hole, and Pal became occupied in trying to calm her down.

What about Jane in all of this, faced with strange and potentially dangerous chimpanzees? She took off running away from the hole, alongside the fence, but in a lolloping gait, putting on a 'play' face and panting in chimpanzee laughter. Why? She was seeking to distract them by inviting them to join her in locomotor play, and amazingly, enough of them did so. As a field worker who was familiar with wild chimpanzees but not so familiar with captive apes, she had spontaneously sized up the situation and acted insightfully.

All ended well, and the chimpanzees were restored to their mended enclosure, but you can guess how our respect for the resourceful Dr Goodall jumped up a few notches!

48 WENNER-GREN

One of the joys and satisfactions of academia is joining in international meetings with top-notch colleagues, often held in interesting places. These gatherings provide face-to-face interaction that can include mind-blowing revelations or the necessary pragmatics of planning research agendas. I was fortunate to take part in many of these, on five continents, at sites ranging from Bali to Lake Turkana, Kenya. The formats ranged from small groups to mass gatherings, and the numbers varied from a handful to thousands, held in major cities or conference centres, even castles. Such meetings are called conferences, workshops, symposia, etc.

In anthropology, the Rolls Royce of such meetings, without a doubt, is a Wenner-Gren symposium. The Wenner-Gren Foundation for Anthropological Research (W-G), based in New York, is a non-profit body dedicated to supporting anthropology, in various ways, for example, the leading journal, *Current Anthropology*. Their discussion meetings are its most exclusive undertaking, being small groups of top academicians (about 20) sequestered for a week. Organised by leaders in a given field, they tackle a target topic from multiple, often inter-disciplinary, perspectives. Participation is by invitation only, and all expenses are paid. W-G holds only two or three such meetings a year, and the proceedings usually are published as an edited book.

What makes these meetings so special? W-G has a formula, almost a script, honed over the decades, the main aim of which is to make the most of the limited time available for maximum exchange of knowledge. For example, each participant submits a paper in advance that is circulated to all participants for reading beforehand. This pre-meeting disclosure allows all to ponder and digest the contents, to be ready for discussion, so no precious time is spent on presentations. Each participant gets an hour devoted to their paper (for contrast, at most conferences, the time devoted to Q&A amounts to 5-10 minutes at most, sometimes none at all). Sequestration means that distractions are kept to a minimum, so that informal discussion continues during meals and late into the evenings. (**49**) For this reason, no guests, students, spouses, etc are allowed (although at one W-G meeting, a participant secreted his spouse in a nearby village and sneaked off to see her).

The W-G meetings are much more than discussion sessions. Much effort is put into making the atmosphere conducive to amicable and rewarding exchanges. Alcohol flows. Meals are sumptuous. Infra-structure is impeccable and flawless. Some evenings offer entertainment, others include jaunts to local sites. Spontaneity also is encouraged, from impromptu stone knapping to late-night bonfires on the beach.

Some aspects are just ingenious. Halfway through the week, given the cumulative effects of intellectual overload, participants get a day off, just to relax and assimilate what they've imbibed. On those days, for example, I've done snorkelling, gone deep sea fishing, hiked in the Alps, and explored a lovely hillside village. At my first W-G meeting, on the last evening, before we all were to disperse the next morning, participants were taken out to the grounds of the castle, where deckchairs were scattered about the lawn. We were snuggled up individually in blankets, offered snifters of brandy and asked to spend some time under the stars, contemplating what we'd experienced over the previous week. In the background, muted classical music drifted out from hidden speakers in the castle's ruined walls. It was magical.

My first W-G meeting was in 1974, held in Burg Wartenstein, a castle in the mountains outside Vienna. The topic was 'The Behaviour of Great Apes'. The second was in 1990, held in the Hotel do Guincho, in Cascais, Portugal. The topic was 'Tools, Language and Intelligence: Evolutionary Implications'. The third was in 1994, held at the Hotel Cabo San Lucas, Baja Mexico. The topic was 'The Great Apes Revisited'. The fourth was in 1999, back at the Hotel Cabo San Lucas. The topic was 'Anthropology at the End of the Century'. Unlike the other meetings, the participants were organisers of previous meetings, for a summing-up not just of the discipline, but of the retiring president's term at W-G, Sydel Silverman. Her book gives details of the meetings, including photographs and Caroline Tutin's limericks, for anyone who wants details.

Silverman, S (2002) *The Beast at the Table. Conferencing with Anthropologists*. Altamira Press, Walnut Creek, CA.

49 DIAN AND ME

As a primatologist specialising in the study of wild chimpanzees, I was encouraged and enabled by Jane Goodall, joining her ongoing research project at Gombe, Tanzania. I also got to know another protégé of the archaeologist Louis Leakey, Dian Fossey, who studied mountain gorillas, mostly in Rwanda. Dian was as unusual, even flamboyant, as Jane was quiet and thoughtful. Dian's book, *Gorillas in the Mist*, described her sometimes unorthodox ways of dealing with poachers who threatened her precious, highly endangered great apes. It was later made into a highly successful Hollywood film, starring Sigourney Weaver as Dian. Years before I met Dian, there were stories, for example, of how she'd arrived at Gombe with a leopard-skin handbag, which greatly excited the chimpanzees.

She and I first met in Austria, at the Berg Wartenstein castle, famously used by the Wenner-Gren Foundation for anthropological conferences (see **48**). Dian arrived hobbling on a walking stick. When asked what was wrong, she casually replied that she had a broken leg. It had fractured from a fall in the Virunga Volcanoes at her remote field site, where she had carried on working until her next scheduled break. That brought her to Vienna, where she had the bones re-set properly before the meeting. She was a tough cookie.

The castle had a lovely old library, which we were invited to make use of for conversations, apart from the conference sessions. One evening, several of us did so, but eventually only four persons remained. Junichiro Itani and Toshisada Nishida sat in one corner, bound up in a seemingly interminable game of Go, oblivious to all else. (Figs. 4, 6) Dian and I sat exchanging stories about our apes, but she had spotted a decanter of brandy on a sideboard. It seemed to demand sampling, but once begun, we carried on, until it was empty. I don't know what time we finally retired to our beds, but it was very late.

I last saw Dian in Atlanta, at a congress of the International Primatological Society, where we had breakfast together in the conference hotel. For some reason, I asked her about a gorilla vocalisation, the so-called pig-grunt. She gave a very audible rendition of it, which attracted a certain amount of attention from fellow breakfasters. Then she required me to follow suit, and it being a new sound for me, it took me several tries to get right, or so she said, by which time, we really were in danger of being thrown out of the dining room.

We corresponded over the years, but my last aerogramme

to her came back undelivered, marked 'return to sender'. It had arrived soon after she was murdered, at her field camp, Karisoke, by persons unknown. It remains in my correspondence files, unopened.

50 CHIMPOLOGISTS AND SPORT

During one of the 'Understanding Chimpanzees' conferences in Chicago, the timing of sessions allowed for attendance at a major league baseball game. Wrigley Field, the home of the Chicago Cubs, is one of only two traditional stadia left in the Major League Baseball, with its idiosyncratic architecture, ivy-covered boundary walls, etc. (Fenway Park, home of the Boston Red Sox, is the other.) So, I asked Toshisada Nishida and Christophe Boesch if they wanted to join me to see a game. The former knew baseball from Japan, but the latter had never seen it played. It turned out that neither was really interested in the game of the day. Compared to football, basketball or ice hockey, baseball's pace is slow and its rules, terms and strategy are opaque. Nishida admitted that what he really wanted was to go to the Cubs' gift shop to buy lots of baseball souvenirs to take back to Japan, especially those relating to Sammy Sosa, a famous home-run slugger for the Cubs. That was easy enough to do. Boesch's boredom was harder to deal with, until a foul ball hit into the stands struck a person in the head, sitting just a few rows in front of us. She collapsed in a heap, requiring medical intervention. This unanticipated risk factor reanimated Boesch's attention, so that we stayed for a few more innings, perhaps because he hoped for more such action, which did not happen. So much for my proselytising about the Great American Pastime.

Sport can be tied to academia in other ways. I learned to time my visits to give research talks to link up with my sporting inclinations. For example, I would request that my talk be on a Monday, so that I could fly in early, over the weekend and run a race on the day before the talk, as most big races are run on Sunday mornings, such as the Jersey Half-Marathon in the Channel Islands. Encouraged by this, I began to enquire if the hosts could provide tickets to local sporting events that happened (!) to coincide with my visit.

John Mitani wangled a ticket for me to see the famed University of Michigan gridiron football team play in The Big House, one of the largest venues in the country, seating over 100,000 fans. I was able to see Syracuse University's basketball team play in the Carrier Dome, the biggest venue for basketball in America. The biggest challenge was to get to see the championship basketball team of Duke University, the Blue Devils, play in perpetually sold-out Cameron arena. Students of the university had to camp out in a queue for days in advance to get a ticket to a big game. My host, Steve Churchill, told me that getting a ticket for me would be impossible, but somehow he managed to come up with a pair. It turned out that he'd gone to the Head of Department, who was willing to sacrifice his and his wife's season tickets on this occasion. The game and atmosphere were tremendous, and afterwards I thanked Steve profusely. He then thanked me just as emphatically, saying he had never seen a Duke game before and never expected to be able to do so again! Such are the acts of sportaholics.

51 MUNRO-BAGGING

The Highlands of Scotland live up to their name by having many mountains, but they pale in comparison to higher altitudes in the European Alps, the Asian Himalayas, South American Andes, or North American Rockies. Instead, Scotland has many smaller and widespread mountains. By long-standing tradition, those peaks with summits above 3000 feet (915 metres) are called Munros, in honour of the first person to list and to ascend all 284 of them. These days, many outdoor-minded folks make a hobby of ascending them, ticking them off the list like a bird-watcher with a 'life-list' of species. These devoted and energetic people are nicknamed 'Munro-baggers'.

I am not one of them, being instead a dilettante, with only a couple of handfuls of Munros to my name. Every one of my successful ascents, and even a few failures, have brought me pleasure, even if at the time, I could not always say so. Often, the satisfaction comes not just from the 'climb', although none of my efforts have included real mountaineering with ropes, but also from the walk into the mountain's base, across scenic burn and bog.

The only Munro that I've done several times is Mt. Keen (3081 ft), at the head of Glen Esk, in Angus. Why? Because it is easily accessible to The Burn, the stately home and estate turned conference centre used annually by many Scottish universities for retreats, such as 'reading parties'. It is the most southerly Munro and the only one with an English name, but that does not mean it's easy. Mt. Keen is roughly conical at the top, strewn with boulders but no single path, vegetation, or other landmark, which means that even in the summer, it can be tricky. If fog rolls in when you are at the summit, without a compass you have no way of knowing in which direction to head for the descent. Failure to choose the right way down might have you wandering over trackless, uninhabited wilderness. It is a low Munro but it can be just as challenging as any higher mountain: Once in a January ascent with some students, the wind became so strong near the summit that we could not stand upright, so we continued on all fours. Even that became impossible, so we had to give up and retreat, with the summit within sight.

Every mountain is different, of course. Schiehallion (3553 ft) is a taller one, standing alone and overlooking scenic Loch Rannoch, but its height is not the challenge. Rather, it has several false summits on the way up, so that your hopes repeatedly rise of nearing the top, only to be dashed when you later realise that there is further to go. The tallest mountain in Scotland, indeed in the British Isles, is Ben Nevis (4409 ft) and it presents a good day's work, requiring 13 miles of walking from and back to the carpark, with ups and downs en route.

As the name indicates, Ben Lomond (3195 ft) is near the famous Loch Lomond, with wonderful views of the lake and the Trossachs. It is near Rowerdennan, another rustic wilderness centre used by universities for reading parties, hence this story…

On a decent winter's day, a mixed party of staff and students set out to bag this Munro. There were about a dozen of us, mostly first- timers, all of whom had been warned about proper clothing and the need for boots. Before we set out, I noted that one of the female students had heeded our advice, but her boots were over-the-knee, brightly-coloured, vinyl fashion boots with thin soles and prominent heels. Another staff member, Helen Ross, and I glanced at each other but said nothing, not wanting to embarrass her in front of her peers.

As we progressed, less fit members of the party began to lag behind and eventually to abandon the climb. The fashionable female kept going as others turned back, but then one of the heels broke off. Surely, she would quit now! She didn't, instead hobbling on, with asymmetric gait. Later, we reached the snowline; the snow was not deep but it made footing more difficult. Surely, she would quit now! Nope, without a word, she kept going. Finally, only five of the party reached the summit, triumphant but cold and tired, and she was one of them. I had not paid much notice to her before, but decades later, I recall her name, Ros Grayson, and not those of the others.

52 GUMMED-UP MARMOSETS

The Callitrichidae, marmoset and tamarin monkeys, are unique, in that they are the only taxonomic family of primates to have litters instead of single offspring. Within the callitrichid evolutionary radiation, the two types are distinguished clearly by their diet. Marmosets are gummivores, that is, they focus their foraging on the secreted exudates of plants, such as saps and resins. To facilitate their feeding, they have prominent, sharp incisor teeth, which they use to gouge 'wells' through the bark of woody plants. These gnawed-out spots allow the secretions to pool in the resulting concavity, to be licked up by the monkeys.

When I took over directing the Primate Unit at Stirling University, I noticed that many of the adult common marmosets were snaggle-toothed, but the youngsters were not, so they had not been born that way. Their cages were made of metal, but had only two components of wood, perches and a sleeping box, which were pock-marked from gnawing. Why did they do so, as nothing nutritional could be gained from these activities?

All of the monkeys were captive-born, so they could not be expressing a hold-over behaviour pattern from the wild, so something else must explain this strong urge to gnaw. Could this habit be an evolved nutritional need for plant gum, which if the opportunity to harvest it is denied, actually prevents their teeth from developing normally? This was too intriguing a mystery to ignore! We found no record of captive marmosets ever having been fed gum before, despite their long-term, common presence in laboratories.

So, if gum is their goal, then we had to give them gum! Where to find it, short of an expedition to the Amazon? Attentive readers will know that plant gum is an everyday part of human diet, being present in ice cream, yoghurt, sweets, etc., as a stabiliser and emulsifier. A specific type, gum arabic, from savanna acacia trees in Africa, is usually used. Enquiries to a confectionery supplier yielded four forms of this gum, from raw chunks to water-soluble powder. We gave all four to the marmosets, and without hesitation they tucked in with gusto, despite having never seen it before. So, the appetite was there!

Next we cut fresh lengths of various types of Scottish woody vegetation and affixed those to the inside of the cages. The monkeys quickly went to work visibly and audibly gnawing away, but with different responses to different types of trees, such as willow *versus* conifer. Impressed by their keenness, we decided to devise an 'artificial gum tree'. We got hardwood doweling, which we cut into barrel-shaped lengths into which we bored four longitudinal, tubular cavities, and one central hole all the way through. The cavities in the segments could then be filled with liquid gum and stacked securely on a central metal rod. The assembled apparatus, oriented vertically, could be clamped to the side of a cage.

We daubed a bit of the liquid gum on the outside of the device, put it in place, and stood back to see what would happen. The monkeys approached, licked at the gum on the surface, then began to gouge. The idea was that continued gouging would tap one of the reservoir cavities, thus encouraging them to persist. When a segment was spent, that is, its cavities drained of their contents, then the exhausted segment could be removed and a fresh one put in its place. So simple, and cheap and easy to make. We should have patented it, but instead we published a report of the discovery. As for the suspected long-term beneficial effects on healthy dental growth, we left that to someone else to pursue.

McGrew WC, Brennan J & Russell J (1986) An artificial "gum-tree" for marmosets (*Callithrix j. jacchus*). *Zoo Biology* 5:45-50.

53 CAPTIVE COTTON-TOPS

Once started on a career of chasing after wild chimpanzees, I never expected to switch study species, much less leave field research, but events dictated otherwise. Stirling had a captive colony of marmosets and tamarin monkeys from South America, who lived in cages on the top floor of the Cottrell Building (see **52**). This building housed mostly faculty offices and teaching areas, making this cheek-by-jowl arrangement highly unusual but conveniently sited. The researcher in charge of the Primate Unit (PU) suddenly left, as did the other primatologist on staff, leaving a colony of monkeys but no one to manage them. The head of department said that unless I took over as director of the PU, he would close it and sell off the monkeys. I acceded, but knew little about these squirrel-sized primates, so it was a fresh challenge.

Luckily, the PU had an experienced and dedicated animal technician staff who were devoted to the monkeys' welfare, although none had specialist training in primatology. The main species, cotton-topped tamarin, was reputed to be difficult, with especially low reproductive success and a reputation for fractious, sometimes fatal, interactions between and even within families. It seemed best to consult Mother Nature.

First, I read all that had been published about the species' ecology and behaviour in the wild, in Colombian rain forest, then about husbandry in other colonies. In nature, they live in extended nuclear families and are highly arboreal and fiercely territorial in nature, making dispersal of offspring a challenge. In the PU, as elsewhere, each family had a separate sparsely-furnished cage, of about 2 m^3 volume, with a single sleeping-box, housing up to about six individuals. All the cages were in one room, lined up facing one another, so they were constantly aroused, threatening and being threatened. It was a recipe for stress that needed to be relieved.

The solution was simple: reclaim all but one of the other rooms in the PU and convert each of them to a territory for only one family. Then add 'furnishing' at multiple levels above the floor, such as tree branches and dangling strips of cloth and rope, enough to give three-dimensional depth, and many routes for approach and avoidance, especially up near the ceiling. The monkeys much preferred being above the humans, rather than at the same level or below them, so we installed multiple shelves, sleeping boxes, and drinking water sources. Thus, they went from 'monkeys per cubic metre' to 'cubic metres per monkey', in an enriched environment. Not a rainforest canopy, but it was an improvement.

But what to do about their now being in isolation from other families, and so from potential mates? The previous director had used translucent, concertina-wired, plastic air conditioning ducting to transfer monkeys from living cage to transport cage. The monkeys readily used this ducting, so why not increase the length to make ducting passages, connecting one room to another or from room to the outdoor enclosure on the roof? The monkeys took to making long-distance journeys throughout the PU, so that soon the corridors were festooned with ducting, with monkeys constantly dashing about to and fro. New behaviours, now enabled, emerged, such as individual monkeys at maturity going prospecting for a mate by visiting neighbouring families.

Many other changes, some apparently trivial, led to

increasingly naturalistic lives. For example, we changed the timing of the PU's lighting system from one geared to the staff's working hours to one that mimicked the annual changes in day-length experienced by their wild counterparts. The monkeys responded by showing us naturalistic seasonality in births. Growing plants in the outdoor area on the roof attracted insects, affording the monkeys opportunities to exercise their predatory skills in insectivory. The result of these modifications was the highest proportion of infant survival of any captive colony of cotton-tops in the world, behaving as 'naturally' as could be accomplished on a Scottish university campus. Left to regulate their own family sizes, the PU had the largest families recorded in captivity, of comparable numbers to that in the wild. Truly, a win-win situation.

P.S. In case you're wondering, all research was observational, and none was invasive. No monkeys were bought or sold. To make the situation clear, we opened the PU to the Scottish Society for the Prevention of Cruelty to Animals (SSPCA) for close inspection, with no resulting problems revealed.

McGrew WC & McLuckie EC (1986) Philopatry and dispersal in the cotton-top tamarin, *Saguinus (o.) oedipus*: An attempted laboratory simulation. *International Journal of Primatology* 7: 399-420.

54 SNAKEBIT

My adolescent interest in herpetology has never waned, but living in UK gives few opportunities for pursuing it. However, Scotland does have one species of venomous snake, an adder.

Once we were at one of the University of Stirling's 'reading party' weekends for undergraduates at The Burn, in Angus. (Fig. 18) On the way back from a walk with students in Glen Esk, I spied a hatchling adder crossing the trail ahead of us. It was tiny, barely a foot long. I decided to catch it, in order to show the students its fangs, etc. Unfortunately, in the process, one of those fangs caught me in the wedding-ring finger. Through embarrassment, I said nothing about this to anyone and carried on to do my impromptu demonstration of dripping fangs, etc.

Later, as we continued the walk, I could feel my bitten finger start to swell up, so I discreetly removed the ring and put it in my pocket. The swelling continued, so I had a quiet word with the oldest student, a post-grad, telling her what had happened and saying that upon return I would retire to my room for the rest of the day, pleading fatigue. I asked her to check on me only if I did not come down to dinner, in case medical intervention was needed. I swore her to strict silence about it, and she agreed. The finger became a bit painful, but a couple of aspirin dealt with that, and I napped.

When I did come down to dinner, the room fell dead silent as I walked in. All eyes were on my hands, but not a word was said until I 'fessed up, and then we all had a good laugh.

55 SHORT-TERM TEACHING

One of the benefits of an academic career is job flexibility. Academics are encouraged to move about, making the most of temporary opportunities arising at institutions other than their current home-base. These peregrinations should be intellectually rewarding but also broaden the mind in general.

Once, when at Stirling University, I did a job-swap with another academic, from the University of North Carolina-Charlotte. The two departments of psychology had set up a simple scheme for semester-long exchanges. The two participants swapped teaching duties, offices, houses, cars, pets, etc., on a comprehensive, trusting basis. Thus, I got a ranch-style suburban house and a station wagon, while my counterpart got an Edwardian flat in a Scottish village and a VW Beetle. My hosting colleagues were hospitable, and the students at UNCC seemed to welcome the novelty. I became very fond of North Carolina, from the Appalachians to the Outer Banks, and its cuisine. I'm surprised that such simple exchange schemes are not more common.

Thrice, I benefited from semester-long hires at colleges or universities that needed replacement teaching for members of staff going on sabbatical leave. First was the Department of Anthropology, at the University of New Mexico, in Albuquerque. It was one of the best such departments in North America, and the appointment was perfectly timed for when I was making the transition from psychology to anthropology. I fell in love with the High Desert, green chilli sauce and the ethnic richness of Native American and Hispanic American cultures.

Then came a stint at Earlham College, in Richmond, Indiana. Earlham is a proto-typical liberal arts college of the highest quality, with Quaker origins. Small and friendly, with keen and inquiring students, taught in small classes. It was my first experience of that sort of academic atmosphere. I became a total convert and would have accepted a permanent appointment if one had been offered. I formed real respect for Quaker culture, based on simplicity, humility, and tolerance, as applied to the higher education setting. Everyone from the president to the janitor was on a first-name basis. Voting was seen as divisive, so decision-making was done consensually. Students participated fully in all decisions, including my hiring; I got more of a grilling at my interview with them, than the one with the faculty!

Finally, I had a semester's teaching at the University of California, Berkeley, one of the highest- ranking universities in the USA. For the first and only time in my career, I taught an 'auditorium class' of almost 300 students. My job was to appear only three times weekly at the podium to lecture, while all the other duties, from marking to seminars, were done by a team of talented graduate students. The city (sometimes known as 'The People's Republic of Berkeley') was a fascinating mix of Nobel Prize winners, who each got a named parking place at the university as a reward, and street people camped out in People's Park. Across the Bay, accessible by BART (Bay Area Rapid Transit) were the many attractions of San Francisco. I even took the opportunity to audit a mammalogy course, in Biological Sciences, from Jim Patton, as I was due to teach that subject back home at Miami University upon my return (see 57).

56 ANDECHS

Beginning in 1993, I spent several summers living and working at the Forschungstelle für Humanethologie, in the village of

Erling-Andechs, Bavaria. It was a sub-unit of the Max-Planck Institut für Verhaltensphysiologie, located only 6 km away at Seewiesen, famous for the pioneering work of the Nobel Prize winner Konrad Lorenz. We went to Andechs to work with its head, Irenaeus Eibl-Eibesfeldt, although more of the time was spent with his number two, my old friend Wulf Schiefenhövel. (Fig. 17)

The institute was on self-contained grounds, based in a miniature but modern castle ('The Schloss'), its social and administrative centre. Nearby were less prominent buildings with accommodations and laboratories, and the most important component, the archive. Eibl and his team had spent decades photographing the lifeways of four traditional cultures, Eipo (Irian Jaya), Himba (Namibia), San (Botswana), and Yanomamo (Venezuela), accumulating hundreds of kilometres on cine film of these 'disappearing' human societies. In that first summer, we spend many hours working through archival footage, extracting data on handedness (see **102**). Although the films had a soundtrack, the tribal languages were unknown to us, but that mattered little, as we focused on their hands in action.

The institute was international in composition, with frequent visits by past members or current students. The social life was lively, for example, every weekday morning at 11 am, there was a 'second breakfast', with coffee, tea, etc. plus fresh pastries from the village bakery, around a big table. Every 4th of July, Linda and I gave a big barbecue for everyone, with grilled sausages of various kinds, baked beans, potato salad, etc. and a keg of local beer (about which, more below). Somehow, there was always music.

However, the most notable social event, reserved for special occasions, was a New Guinea-style pig roast, in an earth oven, orchestrated by Wulf and his colleagues from the Eipo project, with help from his children. Early in the day, a pit was dug while a bonfire heated up cobble-sized stones until they were white hot. The pit was lined with aluminium foil (which should have been banana leaves, but those were in short supply in Bavaria). When the stones were ready, into the pit they went, and on top of them were layered haunches of pork and various root vegetables (e.g. sweet potato) and leafy ones (e.g. cabbage). The aluminium foil was carefully folded over the top and the pit filled in. Depending on the quantity of food and the soil temperature, we waited for a few hours, appetites growing, until the steamed contents of the pit were unearthed and the feast began. Salivation and satisfaction ruled!

The beer came from Andech's local brewery, famous throughout Germany and beyond for its fine brews, served in half or one-litre glass mugs. Kloster Andechs is one of the few remaining monastery breweries in Germany, dating back centuries; it sits atop a hill, with great views of the countryside. It has space for hundreds of customers, both indoors and out, as many come from Munich by S-Bahn, especially on sunny days, to bask and imbibe in the Biergarten. Of course, the day-trippers also can say, if they wish, that they *really* came to see the lovely church in the monastery complex, famous as a site of pilgrimage for persons seeking or celebrating divine help. Or they can claim to come to visit the grave of Carl Orff, composer of 'Carmina Burana', born in Andechs. From the institute to the brewery is a short walk along wooded paths, a route often taken by researchers, when in need of a break.

It's no wonder that I've gone back to Andechs almost every year since then, although 2020 was a rare exception, because of Covid.

Marchant LF, McGrew WC & Eibl-Eibesfeldt I (1995) Is human handedness universal? Ethological analyses from three traditional cultures. *Ethology* 101: 239-258.

57 ARDI AND ME

In the autumn of 1994, Prof. Tim White and colleagues introduced to the world the latest fossil hominid find, *Ardipithecus ramidus*, at a huge press conference at the University of California, Berkeley. The world's media gathered to hear the findings on 'Ardi', as she was nicknamed, who was to become one of the world's most complete skeletons of our extinct relatives. It has to be phrased carefully this way because the published details of the finding were not available until years later, in 2009! At that point, in 1994, I was a visiting professor in the Dept. of Anthropology at Berkeley.

Having avoided the media hoopla, I was walking home at the end of the day, across campus, when approaching on another diagonal sidewalk, about to intersect with me, I saw Tim, pursued by a cameraman and an interviewer with microphone in hand. Presumably he had done too many interviews that day and had had enough. When we converged, Tim suddenly turned to the interviewer and said something like, 'You should interview McGrew, he studies apes!' This caused the interviewer to pause, presumably to ponder the relevance of this assertion, at which point, Tim scarpered around the corner of the Anthropology Museum and disappeared.

So she was stuck with me. We did the interview, and I answered her questions as best I could. I doubt that I said anything useful, but what else could she do? She was from the ABC network affiliate station in San Francisco and presumably needed to go back with something in the can to show to her editor. I admit to wondering how she would deal with the problem of failing to secure her target. The next day at work, several persons grinned at me, inexplicably, before someone explained how she had done so. On the nightly news, I had been presented as Tim White, which apparently solved her problem.

58 STAMPED UPON

My long-time friend and colleague, Prof. Andrew Whiten, and I once published a brief note in *Nature*, the most prestigious scientific journal in the world. But what at first seemed exciting and satisfying turned out to be an embarrassment…

It started when we collaborated on an exhibit on chimpanzee culture at the summer festivities of The Royal Society in London. A member of the public gave to Andy a Liberian postage stamp dating from 1901, which appeared to depict a chimpanzee using a stick tool at a termite mound. This astonished us, though it was plausible, given that Liberian chimpanzees *do* use tools in extractive foraging. It meant that 60 years before Jane Goodall reported tool making and using in termite 'fishing', it already was known, at least in Liberia. So we sent off a revelatory note to the journal, and it was published.

However, soon more information came forth, and it was unexpectedly revealing. First, postage stamps of Liberia then were designed and printed in Europe, so there was no need for a connection to that habitat country in West Africa. Second, the image turned out to be the borrowed use of an already existing engraving, which based on an image from a German zoo. Third, the supposed termite fishing tool was just a stick in the hand of the chimpanzee depicted, with no necessary connection to any kind of tool use. So much for our scientific hubris!

Whiten DA & McGrew WC (2001) Is this the first portrayal of tool use by a chimpanzee? *Nature* 409: 12.

59 CHIMP HAVEN

Entering the present millennium, the US government had jurisdiction over hundreds of captive chimpanzees, mostly confined in the cramped and deprived conditions of biomedical research laboratories. Many of them had been used in studies of infectious diseases, such as HIV-AIDS, and were now of no further use for other research, so were in effect warehoused. A solution was needed, as existing residential facilities, such as Save the Chimps (Florida) and Primate Foundation of Arizona, lacked the funding and other resources to take in an immense load of incomers. The solution came from federal legislation mandating the establishment of accommodation for these 'retirees', to function as a place for the apes to live out their lives undisturbed. Hence the origin of Chimp Haven.

To succeed, this enterprise needed at least two things besides funding: first, a site, preferably in the American south, the climate of which would allow the chimpanzees to be outdoors for as much of the year as possible. The southern USA's weather and populace also made it more economical, in terms of energy and labour costs. Further, the site should be rural and spacious, away from any centre of human population, for both security and public relations reasons. The less money that had to be spent on securing such a site, the more that could be invested in developing naturalistic facilities. Thus, the ideal site would have extensive, natural, wooded vegetation, providing shelter and three-dimensional space for the apes to roam. To find a site that met these specifications was a big ask.

Second, the organisation to develop and manage this task needed to have appropriate expertise and experience of chimpanzees. They also needed to be open to undertaking new challenges, as this was a pioneering effort at creating an innovative naturalistic and nurturing environment.

Chimp Haven was not meant to mimic an expanded zoo or safari park; rather it was meant to be a refuge and sanctuary for our ape cousins who had earned a quiet and happy retirement, having participated in debilitating research. Nor was it to be a research facility, in contrast to the national primate research centres, such as Delta (Louisiana) or Yerkes (Georgia). Here, welfare took precedence over all else. It seemed unlikely that any one person would have the background in all these areas, so a collective effort was needed.

The first element, the site, was provided by Caddo Parish, which included the city of Shreveport, in north-eastern Louisiana. (The parish had nothing to do with religion; in that state, parishes are the equivalent of counties.) Better known for its floating casinos on the Red River, Shreveport was an encouraging surprise, with inhabitants who welcomed the proposal. They offered a site of 200 acres for only a peppercorn lease, which seemed exceptionally generous for a growing city.

On visiting the site, we discovered perhaps why this site was offered. Its next-door neighbour was a low-security correctional facility, that is, a prison, so it was unlikely to be a good bet for a housing development.

Once agreed, I sent a survey team of three students from Miami University to assess the site's ecological characteristics. Their published report of edible plants (pecan, persimmon, etc.) and mature hardwood trees (oak, sweetgum, etc.), in addition to less attractive tracts of pine forest, was positive.

The second element was led by Linda Brent, the only member of the founding team who had ever seen a wild chimpanzee, plus others with extensive experience in the federal facilities from which the apes would come, such as Frans de Waal. I was one of those invited to join the Board of Directors, as the token field researcher. The task of designing the facility was given to a prize- winning designer of zoo exhibits. The result was a compromise of differing opinions, especially on the design of the first big outdoor enclosure, which at 6 acres would be the largest in North America.

Most of my suggestions were ignored, disappointingly, as were the results of the students' survey. The resulting enclosure contained coniferous agro-forestry and had a risky water moat. When another team of Miami students and I censused and tagged the 3000+ trees in it, more than 95% were inedible sticky pine, but to be fair, these trees provided lots of year-round shade.

Prior to the release of the first group of chimpanzees into the enclosure, we tested them with bundles of vegetation of the species growing in it, to see if they would eat or ignore it. Most of them had eaten only pelleted 'chow' and supermarket fruit before and never anything from nature. They showed sensible discrimination, eating some kinds with enthusiasm, others minimally, and one (pine) not at all. One adult female took a bite of pine needles, then spat it out.

After serving for five years, I retired from the Board, as I was moving to England. Thus I missed the grand summer's day when the first group was released into the enclosure, with some encouragement from attractive food, such as watermelon, strewn on the ground before them. The chimpanzees emerged cautiously, but quickly moved into gendered mode, with the females food-grunting and gathering up handfuls of the food, while the males went off pant-hooting on a boundary-patrol, apparently hunting for the strangers that they'd heard before, but never seen. A satisfactory start, it seems.

Horvath J, Cresswell M, O'Malley RC & McGrew WC (2007) Plant species as potential food, nesting material, or tools at a chimpanzee refuge site in Caddo Parish, Louisiana. *International Journal of Primatology* 28: 135-158.

60 MARKETING GREAT APES

In 1994, the Wenner-Gren Foundation for Anthropological Research sponsored a symposium meeting on 'The Great Apes Revisited', in Cabo San Lucas, Mexico (see **48**). It marked the 20th anniversary of a similar conference, 'The Great Apes', held in 1974. Only two of the attendees at the second conference had attended the first, and these 'repeaters' organised its follow-up. Two years later, Cambridge University Press (CUP) published an edited volume of the meeting's presentations, *Great Ape Societies* (*GAS*).

Unlike best-selling books by well-known authors, publishers of academic books rarely hold book launches; rather, they advertise mainly in scientific journals or online. However, in Miami University's primatology group of faculty and students, laboratory chat turned to thoughts of doing more to get the book up and running. Already one of the group's undergraduates, Melanie Peterson, had done illustrations for the book's back cover. They were four portraits of the living types of great ape: bonobo, chimpanzee, gorilla, orangutan.

The group decided to target the next biennial meeting of the International Primatological Society, normally attended by many hundreds of primatologists, to be held in 1996 in Madison, Wisconsin. The plan was to set up a special desk in the book sales area of the conference, featuring just *GAS*. It would be manned by student volunteers wearing specially designed T-shirts portraying the book's back cover, high-lighting Melanie's drawings. Customers who bought the book would be eligible to buy a T-shirt, with all profits from the sales (donations of any amount) to go to four choices of conservation organisations, one each for the four ape species. So, the buyer would walk away with book and T-shirt, and hopefully, wear the latter during the conference, thus providing mobile advertising.

We pitched the plan to CUP, who were sceptical from the outset. When we asked them to bring a large quantity of books to sell at the IPS meeting, they said at first that they would bring more than usual for a new release, that is, a dozen. After explaining our plan in full, they upped that number to 150, making it the largest number of books of one title they'd ever taken to a conference. When we asked them to foot the bill for the T-shirts, they declined, presumably because this was not a normal expense for an academic tome. This didn't stop the students, who knew of a good T-shirt-making firm in the college town of Oxford, Ohio. So, we drove to Madison with boxes full of T-shirts and linked up with boxes full of books. The plan worked splendidly. We sold most of the books and were able to send hundreds of dollars to the four conservation organisations.

Perhaps because of this success, 16 years later, in 2012, CUP agreed to another book launch, at that year's meeting of the American Association of Physical Anthropologists. This launch was to celebrate the publication of Toshisada Nishida's scientific memoir of his long career of studying the chimpanzees of the Mahale Mountains of Tanzania, *Chimpanzees of the Lakeshore*. He had died not long before the book's publication and the conference, so there was a poignancy about the event, attended by a larger than usual number of Japanese primatologists. The launch became a sort of academic wake, fuelled by snack food and draught beer. It was attended by many more persons than expected, who responded warmly to the brief commemorative tributes given. Of course, many of those attending bought the book too.

The event drew so many people that the keg of beer soon ran dry, but more folks kept arriving, spurred by word of mouth. Another keg was quickly ordered; I had to lend the

CUP rep the money to pay for it, as he had exceeded his budget. The only person missing from this spontaneous outpouring of memorial celebration was Nishida-*sensei* himself, and he would have enjoyed it immensely.

61 VERSAILLES HIGH-JINX

Once at a primatological conference sponsored by the Fondation Fyssen, we were put up at the most luxurious hotel in Versailles. At the end of the conference, we adjourned to the bar to relax and celebrate. We could not help but notice that something was in the offing. We asked a member of staff, who told us that the hotel was about to hold an opening event for its brand-new spa, and that Jean Le Pen (the then-leader of the right-wing Front National) would be attending. After a few more drinks, it seemed a good idea for us to try to crash the party, on behalf of the proletariat.

So, four of us set off toward the spa, expecting to be met and denied entry. We gate-crashers were Kim Bard, Paul Garber, Tim Ingold and me. No one said a word to us, and when we got inside the spa, we saw a wonderful setting of plants and fountains, the centrepiece of which was a beautiful swimming pool. Scattered around were small groups of people sipping champagne and eating canapés, but the atmosphere seemed a bit too tame. So we decided to have a swim in the pool, which was unoccupied, which meant we would have it all to ourselves.

We strolled down to the poolside, stripped to our underwear, and in we went. We cavorted and splashed, but no one paid the slightest attention to us. The cosmopolitan Parisians just kept on being cosmopolitan Parisians. I recall a few details: Tim was the only one of us to fold all his clothing into a neat stack. Paul seemed to be the keenest. Kim jumped in and broke her ankle on the pool bottom but toughed it out. (Next day at breakfast, she appeared in a plaster cast, which we all signed.) So, after a while, having failed to make any noticeable impact, we decided that enough was enough, got out, dried off, and got dressed.

Then, just as we were about to leave, we heard that Madame Fyssen was about to arrive. Surely, she must be given a chance to see this! So, we stripped down again and re-entered the pool. She paid no attention to us either, in fact, seemed not recognise us, although we had just been at her conference. Perhaps she was too embarrassed to acknowledge us? So, again we decamped.

By way of follow-up, Paul and I did the spontaneous strip-and-swim thing again a few times, at various conferences, from Bali to Vera Cruz. Sometimes others joined us (but mostly not), and eventually the fellowship of the piscine faded away.

62 STANCES WITH WOLVES

In 2003, I spent several happy months in Hungary, as part of a study group at the Collegium Budapest, a distinguished institute of advanced study. One of our colleagues was the Hungarian ethologist Prof. Adam Miklosi, who studies canine behaviour. We did a field trip to his research station in the woods, where he had wolves, dogs and wolf-dog hybrids. The cross-breeding combination is not unusual, as in many places, such as Italy, the two species hybridise when the wild wolves approach human habitation and meet their domestic counterparts.

After a walking tour around the spacious pens, viewing groups of each type, Adam asked how many of us wanted to go in with the wolves. Surely, he's joking, I thought, but not so. We uneasy volunteers were told to stay calm (!), move slowly with no sudden motions, and remain standing up. We went into the enclosure in a small group, and the wolf pack came trotting over to check us out. One adult approached me, went bipedal and put its forepaws on my shoulders, so that we were face to face, only inches apart. It sniffed me thoroughly, then dropped back down to normal quadrupedality and wandered off. I'd never guessed that wolves could be so tall! One of my colleagues, a palaeo-anthropologist, Iain Davidson, couldn't resist crouching down to examine the many chewed bones on the ground. I took a photo of him scrutinising the bones with a wolf looking over his shoulder, apparently curious to see what interested this human. He survived.

63 NAME GAME

The life sciences engage with millions of types of organisms, and each type requires a universally accepted name, to make sense of all the varied data. Arguably, the most important category is the species, and the naming of species is highly codified. To name a new one, all sorts of criteria must be met, but the most intriguing part of the process is the species half of the binomial, as in *Homo sapiens*. There were several types of *Homo* (the genus) but we humans jealously guard the *sapiens,* for we would not like to be confused with *Homo neanderthalensis!*

Every biologist likely day-dreams of naming a species or of having a species named after them. Luckily, I've had both, although I can take little credit. In the first case, we found a new species of intestinal nematode infecting chimpanzees, while studying the apes at Jane Goodall's study site, Gombe, in Tanzania. We didn't know what we'd found until our parasitologist colleague called it to our attention, after her careful analysis of faecal samples, done later in the laboratory in New Orleans. All we'd done in the field was to collect and preserve ape dung! (see 77) We resisted the temptation to name it after ourselves, which is considered a bit tacky, and combining the names of three persons would be unwieldy. So, we named it *Probstmayria gombensis*, after the field site. Such zoo-geographical naming is common and useful.

My hopes on the second front rose when a former student of mine, Mike Harrison, discovered a new species of monkey in Gabon, Central Africa. New species of living primates are rare, and any primatologist would be thrilled to get the species monicker. Wisely, he chose to name it *Cercopithecus solatus*, or in common language, the sun-tailed guenon, after its yellow-tipped tail. Thus, he took another well-used precedent, which is to name the new species after one of its obvious physical characteristics.

Finally *my* species came to be, near my retirement. It is a species that I've never seen, and likely never will, and if I did, I would probably not be able to identify it accurately. However, it was apt, being a new species of termite. I spent many years of my chimpanzee-chasing career studying those apes preying on termites, using impressive but simple tools. Another of my former students working at Gombe, Robert O'Malley, spotted a novel-looking termite, and he and the entomological expert, Rudolph Scheffrahn, agreed to name it after me. What a thrill! I will treasure their generosity forever. The most obvious physical characteristic of the species is its bulging snout, which is *not* attractive. Hmm...

File SK (1976) *Probstmayria gombensis sp. n.* (Nematoda: Atractidae) from the chimpanzee. *Journal of Primatology* 62: 256-258.

Scheffrahn RH & O'Malley RC (2010) A new termite (Isoptera: Termitidae: Termitinae: *Proboscitermes mcgrewi*), from Tanzania. *Zootaxa* 2670: 52-58.

64 MIAMI TO CAMBRIDGE

Soon after I joined Miami University (not to be confused with the University of Miami, Florida, as Oxford, Ohio, has no sandy beaches nor palm trees!), it began a programme whereby every year a select group of up to eight Miami undergraduates went to the University of Cambridge, England. They studied there for a semester while based at Selwyn College, whose Senior Tutor arranged for their 'supervisions'. This personalised pedagogy, otherwise known as tutorials, entailed fortnightly meetings with a tutor, for one-to-one discussions of essays that the students had been assigned to write. The Miami students had full access to Cambridge's libraries and lectures and lived in private scholars' accommodation. With the students went a permanent member of Miami's faculty to ride herd on these young innocents abroad.

In January 2003, I was that year's selected faculty member, affiliated with Selwyn as a Bye-Fellow and with the Dept. of Biological Anthropology as an academic visitor. My sole teaching duty to Miami was to meet weekly with the students for a seminar, being a discussion of current events in the United Kingdom. In my remaining time, I wrote a book, *The Cultured Chimpanzee*, which turned out to be exceedingly convenient: The book was for Cambridge University Press, so that my assigned editor, Tracey Sanderson, and I could meet to discuss it, chapter by chapter. We easily found a quiet pub that was ideal for lunchtime meetings.

The half-year in Cambridge led to my being offered in 2005 a permanent academic position based in the Leverhulme Centre for Human Evolutionary Studies, which led to a change in Miami's programme. We scaled back the numbers to 2-4 students, as henceforth they would study only anthropology. I took over the task of arranging their supervisions and other needs, thereby replacing the annual requirement for an accompanying Miami faculty member. I arranged for the students to be housed in a college, initially at Downing and later at Corpus Christi, so that they could have the full collegial experience, especially the extra-curricular ones, such as formal hall. They prospered in these arrangements: All achieved high marks on the same scale as Cambridge students, several did publishable individual projects, and some went on to do doctoral study, one of whom stayed on at Cambridge to do so.

All in all, all-round serendipity!

65 FLAKEY ACTIONS

My last research trip to Africa was in 2016, to join in a workshop on the evolutionary origins of human technology, held at the Turkana Basin Institute, Lake Turkana, Kenya, and hosted by Richard and Meave Leakey. Most of the participants were palaeo-anthropologists and archaeologists, but a few others from cognate disciplines were invited to join in, including this chimpanzee-chaser. Basically, I was there thanks to the apes, who use stone tools in nature, although they are not known to make them.

The stars of the event were Sonia Harmand and colleagues, who'd recently presented new findings on stone tools that were 700,000 years older than any previously found. Their discovery was the Lomekwian lithic industry, excavated from a ravine in West Turkana. The unexpected find featured prominently in the media, for at 3.3 million years ago, the only known hominins (extinct forebears of modern humans) had brains no bigger than those of living African apes. Thus, at least in principle, the simple flaked cores of the Lomekwian could have been made by apes. Also, the two techniques by which the Lomekwian was made, as reconstructed via reverse engineering by the archaeologists, are both in the behavioural repertoires of living wild chimpanzees. Hence my presence at the workshop – thanks again to the apes.

For what purpose had the Lomekwian stone tools been used? One candidate function was butchery, but could these crude lithics do the job? To test this, workshop participants were told to make as best they could Lomekwian-like tools and then to use them to butcher a goat. I hasten to add that the goat was to be killed anyway, for dinner; we just had access to it before the cooks. Some of the group demurred, but I ended up with the task of disconnecting a forelimb, while another primatology colleague, Tiago Falotico, had the other one. With our flakes, we set to work, but a sort of unspoken competition quickly emerged, to see which of us could detach first his assigned foreleg. The cutting edge of the flake worked well to slash through skin and muscle, but ligaments and tendons were harder, especially when the fatty tissues made the tools more slippery to hold and tricky to manoeuvre without cutting oneself in the process. We succeeded, and a scientific point was made, at least in terms of feasibility. (Fig. 28)

66 HIGH TABLE

Universities vary greatly. Two of the most unusual are Oxford and Cambridge, in England. They are hyper-collegiate institutions, composed of 30+ constituent colleges that are fiercely independent and have more combined wealth than the university to which they are affiliated. In both of them, the relationship between the colleges and the university is one of mutual co-dependence. The colleges supply the students and their accommodation; the university supplies the degrees and some key facilities, such as laboratories.

Given this longstanding symbiosis, fellowship in a college for academic staff is important although not required, and most enjoy the privileges and pleasures of college membership, which is by invitation only. I was a Fellow of Corpus Christi College, Cambridge, for seven years until my retirement. A cultural anthropologist could do an ethnographic monograph about college life, especially in the older colleges which had medieval origins. As an example of college customs, I describe evening dining at high table.

High table at Corpus refers literally to a single, long table in the Hall, available for dining to fellows and some non-academic staff of the college, and occasionally a limited number of their guests. At the older colleges, the table is literally raised above the floor of the rest of the room where the students and other staff sit. At Corpus, that elevation was only 6 inches, but there was a world of difference between those two heights.

Evening dining is essentially a three-act play. The first act occurs when fellows and their guests assemble before the meal in the Senior Common Room, often for a glass of sherry. All college members wear black academic gowns. Its purpose is to make introductions if there are guests joining the fellows for dinner. When the butler rings a gong, the diners file into the hall, to sit where they please at the high table, that is, seating is not assigned, although guests are expected to sit with their hosts. However, the presiding (senior) fellow, or the Master of the college, takes the head of table, and occupation of the two choice seats to either side of them is the head's purview. The presiding fellow then says a designated Christian grace, in Latin, and all sit down. One of the most anxious moments in my life was the first time that I was presiding fellow, because this function for the evening is assigned just by seniority. Needless to say, I made a complete hash of the Latin pronunciation.

The second act is the meal, served by a team of college staff led by the college butler. There are three courses, starter, main, and dessert, each with an appropriate type of wine. Corpus had a wine cellar of about 13,000 bottles, continually being renewed by the Wine Steward, one of the most important college offices. The menu is fixed, so anyone with dietary requirements or preferences must make them known in advance. The meal is consistently delicious, as colleges vie to have a reputation for serving the best food.

More important than the food, however, is the conversation. After all, anyone can get a good meal at a good restaurant. During the meal, you are expected to chat with five others, being the persons to your left and right, the person directly opposite, and the persons sitting to the left and right of that person opposite. Experienced diners are erudite and entertaining, skills acquired by practice and observation. Topics range vastly, from serious to amusing to ridiculous, but certain potentially fractious topics are meant to be avoided, such as politics and religion. The aim is for a small group of intelligent, knowledgeable persons to have mutually satisfying and stimulating conversations, especially by being generous and thoughtful. This atmosphere is especially important for the guests, who may be complete strangers dining for the first time in such a context and so a bit nervous. The meal ends with another, briefer benedictory grace.

The third act now commences, and it is the most unusual, and the one that most guests find most memorable. It is called Combination, and it takes place in another, private room, especially designated for this purpose, called the Combination Room. No staff are involved once it's underway. There is an even bigger table, and again the presiding fellow takes its head. Diners are encouraged to find new conversation partners, and by now, many guests are adventurous enough to strike out on their own, seeking new topics and acquaintances. All of the conviviality is made easier by various dishes of sweets, nuts, cheese, biscuits, etc, accompanied by three types of alcoholic drink, being port, madeira and claret. (No beers or spirits ever make an appearance here.) These libations are in distinctively-shaped decanters, which circulate continuously around the table. They are passed from right to left (for no obvious reason), and anyone who neglects to keep them moving is gently reminded to do so. Some leave early, others stay as late as they wish, munching, sipping and chatting. Most participants find it the most enjoyable part of the evening.

When I first arrived in Cambridge, Combination included smoking, and the room became smoky, especially if cigars were lit. Instead, there is a nicotine alternative on offer, snuff, which is just dried tobacco pulverised and scented. Corpus had the most wondrous snuff container, an aurochs horn with silver and bejewelled filigree and lid. Attached to it by silver chains were four little tools. Only one of these is strictly necessary, the tiny scoop for transferring a portion of snuff to one's natural 'snuff-box', being that depression formed between fully extended thumb and forefinger, on the back of the hand. To take snuff, you raise the hand to each nostril in turn, taking up a strong sniff. The result is instant pleasure. I confess to having become devoted to this habit and kept several types of snuff in my college room. The fourth tool was a rabbit's foot, for brushing off the hand any stray particles.

Actually, there can be a fourth act, purely personal, which is to ask one or more fellow diners back to your college room, which is a sitting room, not a bedroom, with comfortable couch and easy chairs, for a nightcap. Then spirits such as whisky (in my case, single malt scotch) or cognac come into their own, perhaps accompanied by a bit more snuff. An evening of decadence to be sure.

67 GRAPE EXPECTATIONS

In academia, it is not uncommon for pairs of universities to be fierce competitors, beyond the academic realm. Consider Harvard vs. Yale, or Stanford vs. California-Berkeley, on the gridiron. The greatest such competition may be between Cambridge (Light Blue) and Oxford (Dark Blue), if for no other reason than their antiquity, being hundreds of years old. Their competitive matches cover a wide range of sports, and these occur annually as Varsity Matches, for which the participants earn prized Blues. Not surprisingly, rugby football is one of the biggest of these, though in media terms the Boat Race (eights rowing) on the Thames in London gets more coverage. But arguably the strangest form of competition, known only for these two universities, so far as I know, is in wine-tasting.

Hedonic wine-tasting is common in Oxbridge. All colleges hold these events regularly; my college, Corpus Christi, has one each term, in which up to 25 wines are placed on tables in the Senior Common Room. Around these, fellows and their guests circulate, sipping, swirling, and spitting, with some taking notes. Obtaining the wines is the task of the Wine Steward, whose skills must include entrepreneurial savvy, for this job requires playing the long game. This year's vintages are laid down and may get drunk only years later, after the current steward's term has ended. By tradition,

Corpus specialises in port, in which the wine steward must be a successful wheeler-dealer.

How to make wine-tasting competitive? During my time as a Bye-Fellow at Downing College, I was befriended by Richard Stibbs, who, in addition to his academic post, coached the Cambridge University Wine-Tasting Team. When the Varsity Match was upcoming, he tested potential competitors under match conditions by inviting fellows along to emulate competition under stress, just as in any other sport. We were supposed to show murmurs of approval when they succeeded and disappointment when they did not, thus providing a semblance of the pressure under which they must perform.

Each of the four best candidates for the team was given each wine to taste; there were six reds and six whites, so each individual got 12. The wines were in identical crystal carafes, so the tasting was completely 'blind'. To score maximally, the contestant must identify the grape, country of origin, and vintage. The first was the easiest, but it did not necessarily link to the country of origin, for example, Chile produces some fine wines from the same type of grapes as France. The latter was really tough—how to know whether it was a 1992 or 1993?

After the training session, Richard would take them through each wine, providing clues to the important distinctions between them. Given this sort of practice, it's not surprising that Cambridge won many more matches than did Oxford.

The reader may wonder about what the audience got out of this. As wine-tasters take only a swallow, much wine still remained in the carafes, and it was not going to be poured down the drain. We attendees were tasked with finishing it off!

68 BOOKMAKING

Everyone knows that academics are meant to write books, but many never do, and even those that do get published rarely make any public impact. Mostly, we write for one another, as scholars, in our collective global attempts to advance knowledge. I've written or edited eight books, mostly published by university presses that altogether have sold only a few thousand copies. Thus, J.K. Rowling probably sells more books in an hour than I did in a decades-long career.

Since you'll never see my books in an airport book rack, I'll briefly describe them here:

My first book, *An Ethological Study of Children's Behavior* (1972), was published by pure chance. It originated as my first PhD thesis, written only to obtain the necessary career credentials. A chance coffee-time conversation with a sabbatical visitor from the USA, David Palermo, led to his offering to publish it in the Child Psychology Series, which he edited. It was a breeze, misleadingly easy! It had positive reviews in *Nature*, *Science*, etc. and got translated into Italian and Japanese.

My second book came decades later, *Topics in Primatology, Volume 1. Human Origins* (1992), of which I was one of five editors. It represents a standard type of academic book, being the proceedings of a conference, in this case a session at the congress of the International Primatological Society, in Japan. Like most such edited volumes, it is rarely cited, except by specialists.

My third book is the most important, *Chimpanzee Material Culture* (1992), and it was written deliberately to be both a PhD thesis and a book. It served as my entree into anthropology and won the 1996 WW Howells Prize of the American Anthropological Association, as the best book of the year in biological anthropology. It was reviewed widely in both academic (*Science*) and popular periodicals (*Scientific American*), went into four printings, and was translated into Japanese and Slovenian.

My fourth book, *Chimpanzee Cultures* (1994), was another edited volume, derived from a chimpology conference in Chicago. Four of us shared editorship, including two luminaries of primatology, Richard Wrangham and Frans de Waal. It got a range of good reviews, from *Science* to the *Los Angeles Times*, and, unusually for a conference proceedings, went into paperback within a year.

My fifth book, *Great Apes Societies* (1996) was the most enjoyable edited volume of all, as it arose from a productive and convivial conference in Cabo San Lucas, Mexico. It brought together researchers on all four great ape species. The book got good reviews in general (*Nature*), and specialist (*Evolutionary Anthropology*) scientific journals, as well as the popular press (*BBC Wildlife*).

My sixth book, *The Cultured Chimpanzee* (2004) frankly was disappointing, in terms of lower-than-hoped-for sales and impact. It was meant to present my considered but sometimes provocative views on a key topic of enduring interest (see, for example, Nicolas Langlitz's *Chimpanzee Culture Wars*, 2020, Princeton University Press). Perhaps potential readers suspected that it might overlap too much with the earlier *Chimpanzee Material Culture* (it didn't). It got some good reviews (*Nature*), but the best surprise was for it to be translated into Turkish.

My seventh book, *Chimpanzee Behavior in the Wild* (2010) was co-authored, and my part was the least of the five authors. Basically, my job was to edit the English and to check the comparisons made with the Western scientific literature. It was Toshisada Nishida's next-to-last writing project and included two DVDs with excellent footage illustrating chimpanzee behaviour patterns. The key word was in the subtitle, 'encyclopedia', as it was meant to be a comprehensive, illustrated reference work for chimpologists, but the publisher set too high a purchase price for it to reach its intended targets, students as well as professionals. A lost opportunity.

My eighth book, *Building Bridges between Anthropology, Medicine and Human Ethology* (2011) exemplifies a unique genre, the *Festschrift*, in which a revered and influential academic is celebrated by colleagues contributing to an edited volume. The recipient of this admiration is named in the sub-title, and the book celebrated Wulf's official retirement from the Max-Planck-Gesellschaft. Such books never achieve high sales but their rarity is a measure of the esteem in which their honoree is held. Very few academics receive a *Festschrift*!

The books' details are given below, in case the reader wants to rush to Amazon and order.

McGrew WC (1972) *An Ethological Study of Children's Behavior*. New York: Academic Press, 268 pp.

Nishida T, McGrew WC, Marler P. Pickford M & de Waal FBM (eds) (1992) *Topics in Primatology, Volume 1. Human Origins*. Tokyo University Press, 475 pp.

McGrew WC (1992) *Chimpanzee Material Culture: Implications for Human Evolution*. Cambridge University Press, 277 pp.

Wrangham RW, McGrew WC, de Waal FBM & Heltne PG (eds) (1994) *Chimpanzee Cultures*. Cambridge, MA: Harvard University Press, 424 pp.

McGrew WC, Marchant LF & Nishida T (eds) (1996) *Great Ape Societies*. Cambridge University Press, 328 pp.

McGrew WC (2004) *The Cultured Chimpanzee: Reflections on Cultural Primatology*. Cambridge University Press, 248 pp.

Nishida T, Zamma K, Matsusaka T, Inaba A & McGrew WC (2010) *Chimpanzee Behavior in the Wild: A Visual Encyclopedia*. Tokyo, Springer, 255 pp.

Bruene M, Salter F & McGrew WC (eds) (2011) *Building Bridges between Anthropology, Medicine and Human Ethology: Tributes to Wulf Schiefenhövel*. Bochum University Press, 266 pp.

69 HONORARINESS

In 2011, I retired from my university professorship at Cambridge, as then, retirement at age 67 years was obligatory. This change of status meant changing from a full-sized office to a half-sized one, as I continued teaching biological anthropology on only a part-time basis. It also meant moving most of a sizable library of books and reprints to my other office at Corpus Christi College, and shifting my scientific journals to the library in the Leverhulme Centre for Human Evolutionary Studies. As is customary, I was given emeritus status, that is, Emeritus Professor of Evolutionary Primatology.

I carried on at Corpus until 2016, as Director of Studies for Biological Anthropology, being responsible for undergraduates reading that or related subjects. I also continued college chores, such as admissions interviews. At Oxbridge, all applicants for undergraduate studies are interviewed, a labour-intensive process. The college also had obligatory retirement for its fellows, at age 70 years. Had Corpus offered me Life Fellow status, I could have stayed on to use the workspace provided for Life Fellows, but it did not. I gave away most of my books and reprints (>12,000 of the latter) to former students; most of them ended up in a newly established library in Oxford, in the Institute of Cognitive and Evolutionary Anthropology, thanks to Susana Carvalho.

So, a choice had to be made. The alternatives were to stay on in Cambridge, move to Japan, or return to Scotland. The latter choice was an easy one, so I set about considering how to maintain an academic connection north of the border in retirement. I'd had good experiences at three Scottish universities earlier in my career: Edinburgh, Stirling, and St Andrews. Edinburgh was out because I was fed up now with city life. Stirling had been my longest stint (1973-1992) and I was grateful for the good years spent there, but they no longer had anthropology and would offer me only an honorary readership (the rank I'd held when I left there). So I opted for St Andrews. I'd spent only two summers there, but the academic staff was full of old friends and stimulating colleagues, often one and the same persons. Also, St Andrews was a rising star in UK academia: For the last two years, it has finished second in *The Guardian*'s annual University Rankings, splitting the previous long-standing domination of the top two positions by Oxbridge.

Happily, former colleagues supported my return, and I was interviewed by the Head of the School of Psychology and Neuroscience, Keith Sillar. This move in itself was a form of closure, as psychology was the discipline of my first PhD, decades earlier. On offer was an Honorary Professorship, which entailed designated workspace and access to all School facilities, such as computing, printing, etc., and most usefully, a parking permit! No teaching was required (though I have done a little) and no salary (which was not needed). Now, I am happy as a clam (whatever that metaphor means).

The icing on the cake came when Andy and Susie Whiten found a lovely house for us to buy in a tiny hamlet, nine miles west of St Andrews.

Fig 1 Gombe chimpanzee Humphrey naps in day-nest,
1972 (Photo by WCM)

Fig 2 Gombe leaf party, Upstairs Camp, (l to r): Mark Leighton, WCM,
Stella Brewer, David Riss, Henry Klein, 1973 (Photo by Caroline Tutin)

Fig 3 Gombe chimpanzee Fifi fishes for termites with grass blade, 1973
(Photo by WCM)

Fig 4 Toshisada Nishida (r) and WCM (l) at Takagoyama study site of Japanese
macaques, 1974 (Photo by Caroline Tutin)

Fig 5 Caroline Tutin brings home the bananas, Mahale Mountains, Tanzania, 1975 (Photo by WCM)

Fig 6 Junichiro Itani and WCM on the Lake Tanganyika beach, Mahale Mountains, with Mt Nkungwe in the background. 1975 (Photo by Caroline Tutin)

Fig 7 Assirik landscape, dry season, with leafless baobab trees in centre, 1976
(Photo by WCM)

Fig 8 Pamela
Baldwin with a very
low chimpanzee
nest, Assirik, 1976
(Photo by WCM)

Fig 9 WCM seeks to persuade Stella Brewer's rehabilitating chimpanzees
(l to r: Bobo, Nini, Yula) to eat wild food (*Parkia biglobosa* beans), Assirik,
1976 (Photo by Caroline Tutin)

Fig 10 WCM scales
poacher's ladder of
bamboo to honey-bees'
nest in baobab tree,
Assirik, 1977 (Photo by
Caroline Tutin)

Fig 11 Assirik camp in wet season, one of five huts, 1977 (Photo by WCM)

Fig 12 Chimpanzee Goldilocks cracks palm nuts with hammer-stone (in right hand) and anvil, Little Bassa River, Liberia, 1985 (Photo by Alison Hannah)

Fig 13 Caroline Tutin (l) and Elizabeth Williamson (r) process chimpanzee
faecal samples, Lope-Okanda, Gabon, 1990 (Photo by WCM)

Fig 14 Linda Marchant beside *Macrotermes* termite mound, Gombe, 1992
(Photo by WCM)

Fig 15 Fellow field workers back home in Scotland. l to r: Caroline Tutin, Elizabeth Williamson, Pamela Baldwin, Anthony Collins, Rebecca Kormos, Elizabeth Rogers, 1995 (Photo courtesy of Elizabeth Williamson)

Fig 16 WCM caught lying down on the job, watching chimpanzees in forest canopy overhead, Nimba Mountains, 2007. (Photo by Kathelijne Koops)

Fig 17 Wulf Schiefenhövel (r) and WCM (l) watching chamois on hillside after coming down from ascent of Tyrolian alp, Austria
(Photo by Wulf Schiefenhövel)

Fig 18 Four founders of Scottish Primate Research Group at The Burn, Angus. L to r: Richard Byrne (St Andrews), WCM (Stirling), Elizabeth Rogers (Edinburgh), Andrew Whiten (St Andrews), 2006. (Photo courtesy of SPRG)

Fig 19 Elementary chimpanzee technology: leaf sponge used to dip drinking water from dug well, Semliki, Uganda, 2006. Top: plucked but unused leaves: Middle: processed leaves with veins discarded: Bottom: disentangled leaves from used sponge. (Photo by WCM)

Fig 20 Mahale chimpanzee Primus eats salad with his red colobus monkey meat, Tanzania, 2007 (Photo by Agumi Inaba)

Fig 21 Caroline Phillips collects fresh chimpanzee faeces from forest floor
(centre of picture), Kanyawara, Uganda, 2008 (Photo by WCM)

Fig 22 Paco Bertolani beside chimpanzee nest in papyrus swamp,
Kanyawara, Uganda, 2008 (Photo by WCM)

Fig 23 Freepressionist (filly) with syndicate owners, after her win at Wolverhampton, WCM furthest left (Photo by Craig Bickley)

Fig 24 Susana Carvalho with collected *Parinari* nuts, abundant but uneaten by chimpanzees, Issa, 2012 (Photo by WCM)

Fig 25 Kanyawara chimpanzee line up to do Grooming Hand Clasp; pair in front includes an individual lacking hand, Kibale, Uganda, 2013

(Photo by Kathelijne Koops)

Fig 26 'Fish-in' party of chimpanzees at *Macrotermes* termite mound, Gombe, observed by Rob O'Malley, 2014
(Photo courtesy of Robert O'Malley)

Fig 27 WCM with boa constrictor, Serra da Capivara, Brazil, 2015
(Photo by Agumi Inaba)

Fig 28 Tiago Falotico (r) and WCM (l) use Lomekwian-style flaked stone
tools to detach forelegs of goat, Turkana Basin Institute, Kenya, 2016
(Photo courtesy of TBI)

Fig 29 Four key researchers of chimpanzee shelters (nests): (a) Adriana
Hernandez-Aguilar (Issa), (b) Kathelijne Koops (Nimba), (c) Fiona Stewart
(Fongoli, Nimba), (d) David Samson (Semliki), 2020
(Photos courtesy of AH-A, KK, FS, DS)

Fig 30 The University High School letter jacket still fits the author
60 years later, 2020 (Photo by Agumi Inaba)

FIELDWORK

70 RAVENGLASS

My first field experience as a student at Oxford was with black-headed gulls on the coast of Cumberland (now Cumbria), in early 1966. The gulls nested on the sand dunes in February, in the face of cold onshore winds off the Irish Sea. My project was chosen by my supervisor, Prof. Nikolaas Tinbergen. It entailed burying devices in the sand next to the birds' nests, to be controlled remotely by me from a nearby hide. Each of the devices was a simple mechanical model of a gull's head, which when it emerged from an aluminium box, would do simple head movements. The hide was a one-metre square cube of canvas tent, in which I huddled with my control panel. I was meant to record the birds' response to the models' varied movements. Simple enough.

The birds did not mind the hide, but they were disturbed if a human walked into the colony and then disappeared within it, so I was escorted in by another researcher, deposited in the hide, and then retrieved later after a pre-set interval of a few hours. The birds apparently knew little arithmetic, as they didn't mind that two persons arrived but only one left, or vice versa.

In principle, I then went to work. In practice, what often happened was that some or even all of the devices failed to work, as their mechanisms became jammed by windblown sand. Often this disappointment was clear after only a few minutes, as I fruitlessly worked my way through the options on the control panel to no avail. All I could do then was to sit and wait to be rescued at the appointed time. I soon learned to take a book with me.

Days of frustration passed, and the accumulated data were few. Then, to top it all off, a fierce gale blew all the nests away, and the gulls had to start all over again! Ditto for me. This was the last straw, so I packed it in. Thus, my first experience of birds in the field was an abject failure!

Later I learned that the same project had been tried and then rejected by a previous student, and then by another after me. I somehow doubt that it ever got done.

71 CAYO SANTIAGO

Having done a PhD on an ethological study of children's behaviour, I was set for a career as a developmental psychologist. So why did I abandon that for primatology? I blame it on Charles Darwin. In the latter stages of writing up my thesis, I read his *Expression of the Emotions in Man and Animals*, which drives home the basic point that humans *are* apes, by making convincing comparisons. Having been trained originally as a zoologist, I could not ignore the temptation to have a look at our nearest living relations, the other primates. My plan was to take out a year or two as a post-doctoral primatologist before returning to human beings. Funding was secured for a study of green monkeys in Barbados.

The challenge was my being a total neophyte, but it was solved by getting the opportunity to take part beforehand in the first (and only) Wenner-Gren Foundation field school in primatology. The invitation came from Dr Donald Sade, director of the school, to be held at the Caribbean Primate Research Center, in Puerto Rico, thus providing access to that part of the tropics. The school was to be held at the Center's main field site, on the south coast of the island, Cayo Santiago, an islet occupied by over 700 rhesus macaques. These Old World monkeys were a transplanted population, introduced in the 1930s from India, but they had adapted completely to this paradisical isle. There they had no predators nor diseases and a constant supply of provisioned food, so they thrived and reproduced prolifically.

The school got off to a subdued start in the seaside village of Punta Santiago. We were only six students, some pressed into the service at the last minute to make up the numbers. Only two of the six, David Taub and I, later went on to become established field primatologists. The centre had no accommodation, so we four male students shared a single, small room, while the two female students were shoehorned into the small home of a researcher. There was no kitchen in the laboratory, so meals were a challenge; its refrigerator housed both our food and monkey carcasses. Subsistence was strictly do-it-yourself, so we learned basic cooking from David. Yet the quaint village was on the beach and beer was there to be drunk in the evenings as the sun set over the Caribbean, so somehow we managed.

Classes on theory were held in the lab, but learning in practice took place on the islet, which was a short boat ride away from the mainland. We went out in the mornings, with our packed lunches, and stayed till the late afternoons, each of us assigned to a troop. The monkeys ranged freely everywhere and were well-used to humans walking about among them; each individual was identifiable by a tattooed number on its chest and inner thigh. We learned field techniques, especially for behavioural observations, from square one and applied them to the readily-accessible monkey subjects. In six weeks, I was hooked and never went back to studying humans, with no regrets over the ensuing 50 years spent chasing monkeys and apes instead.

I never made it to Barbados, which is another story, but in 1976 I did meet up in West Africa with the historical source populations of those transplanted green monkeys, when we began the SAPP study of primates at Mt. Assirik in Senegal. There my PhD student, Michael Harrison, did the first comprehensive study of the species' behaviour and ecology.

72 CHIMPOLOGY 'S SCOPE

A recent poll of the public showed Jane Goodall to be the second-most famous woman scientist of all time, after only Marie Curie. This public recognition is based on Jane's pioneering studies of wild chimpanzees at her field-site of Gombe, in Tanzania, East Africa. That project is now 60+ years old, and if one were to draw up academic genealogies, many practitioners of field chimpology would feature in it, as her scientific descendants. I am one of them.

Gombe is only one of over 140 field-sites in sub-Saharan Africa where chimpanzees have been studied. The species ranges from Senegal (the westernmost country in Africa) to Tanzania (which borders on the Indian Ocean), spanning more than 25 countries along that east-west continuum. Why so many sites and how much variation among them? To answer these questions requires more specificity.

In principle, a field-study could last five days, or weeks, months, years, or decades. Any of these time-frames could yield scientifically publishable data, but the feasible questions would differ greatly. In five days, you might be able to collect enough faecal samples to allow DNA extraction that would enable you to characterise an important gene complex in a population. At the other extreme, five or more decades might be necessary to know if a cultural aspect of elementary technology was evolving from generation to generation.

Only 13 study sites (Bossou, Budongo, Bulindi, Fongoli, Gombe, Goualougo, Issa, Mahale, Kalinzu, Kanyawara, Ngogo, Sebitoli, Tai) have fully accessible (habituated, **74**) subjects of study, that is, fewer than 10%. Why so few? Because it takes years of patient, dedicated work to achieve the necessary level of confidence between human and ape. Shorter studies tackle unhabituated to partly habituated populations and start with ecology (vegetation, climate, predators, etc.) based on *indirect* data, that is, the context and products of behaviour, left behind as traces. Thus, early-stage field data resemble those in archaeology more than ethology. With perseverance and luck, the data progress to more and more *direct* (observational) records of daily activity, shown by identifiable individuals who can be followed lifelong. For the record, I worked at nine sites along the continuum, and each one brought different rewards. (**73**)

When I went back to Gombe in 2012, 40 years after my first stint there, I met up again with Sparrow. In 1972, she had been an adolescent female chimpanzee; now she was an aged matriarch. At our first meeting upon 'reunion', her younger companions stared, but her glance at me was brief, as if to say "Oh, it's you again, but you've aged a bit!"

McGrew WC (2017) Field studies of *Pan troglodytes* reviewed and comprehensively mapped, focusing on Japan's contribution to cultural primatology. *Primates* 58: 237-258.

73 *PAN* PLACES

Two main strategies exist for spending a lifetime of chimpanzee-chasing: *depth* or *breadth*. Those who commit to the former found a single study-site and devote their careers to it, following generation after generation of the apes. The archetypal such site is Gombe, studied for 60+ years by Jane Goodall and her team. Those who choose the latter work peripatetically at several sites, drawing comparisons, picking their sites according to specific questions that can be answered there. Each approach has its pros and cons, but both are needed for understanding our species' nearest relations. Over 40 years, I opted for breadth, although I once tried depth for four years at Mt. Assirik. In the process, I gained insights from 13 study sites, scattered across Africa. I worked (marked by a W below) at nine of the 13, with work defined as collecting publishable data, but made only scientific visits to the other four. Seven of the 13 sites offered fully habituated subjects for study, while the other six had varying degrees of habituation (see **78**). I believe that this range of accumulated experiences exceeds in scope those of others who have done chimpanzee field research. Here are some thumbnail descriptions of those places, listed alphabetically:

1   *Assirik* (Senegal, W) Highly seasonal savanna with annual bushfires, full range of large mammal fauna, from lion to

elephant. Isolated and most primitive conditions: grass-thatched huts with bamboo walls, earthen floor, creek water, firewood cooking, no electricity. My favourite site, for all these reasons! Founded by Stirling African Primate Project (SAPP). (see **90-96**) (Fig.16)

2   *Belinga* (Gabon, W) Equatorial rain forest. Totally unhabituated chimpanzees and gorillas. Abandoned mining camp with derelict villa housing, wood-fired hot baths, fruit trees (e.g. avocado) on doorstep, site shared with pygmy guides, thus my only experience of day-today working with hunter- gatherers. Site found by Caroline Tutin and Michel Fernandez. (**75, 83, 98**)

3   *Bossou* (Guinea) Sacred wooded hills surrounded by horticulture, nearby village, 'outdoor laboratory' for field experiments, small and declining community of apes. Chimpanzees are expert nut-crackers, using stone hammers and anvils. Provides the most daily human-ape interaction, for better or worse. Founded by Yukimaru Sugiyama, later headed by Tetsuro Matsuzawa.

4   *Fongoli* (Senegal, W) Savanna chimpanzees in open, unprotected area, close to major town, where researchers lived. Depauperate fauna replaced by local livestock. Apes shared drinking water with locals in dry season, from a tiny spring. Ingenious tool-users, including stick 'spears' to hunt bush-babies. First habituated population of savanna chimpanzees, by Jill Pruetz and Paco Bertolani.

5   *Gombe* (Tanzania, W) Small national park on eastern shore of Lake Tanganyika. Served by public transport ('water-taxis'), visited daily by tourists. Biological

'island' surrounded by human small-holding horticulture (shambas). Achingly beautiful, from sun rising over the crest of the Albertine Rift, terrain sweeping down to pebble beaches, with crystal-clear water for swimming and spectacular sunsets over the lake. Full facilities, so qualifies as a resort as well as research site! Most productive and often-cited field study of chimpanzees, founded by Jane Goodall (see **82**). (Fig. 2)

6   *Issa* (Tanzania, W) Newest long-term chimpanzee study site. Savanna woodland in unprotected area inland from Lake Tanganyika. Easily reached by road. Tented accommodation but fully staffed and integrated, with facilities for student groups. High-tech facilities from satellite-phones to drones. Full range of sympatric mammals, including large predators. Founders: Alex Piel and Fiona Stewart (**75**).

7   *Kanyawara* (Uganda) Long-standing facilities with prestigious (Harvard) university-base, in Kibale National Park. Exceptional infrastructure and convenient logistics nearby at Fort Portal. Chimpanzees range from forest to papyrus swamp, but also some crop-raiding. Broad range of ecological and ethological topics of research, plus physiological substrates, studied non-invasively. Developed by Richard Wrangham (**80**). (Figs. 21, 22)

8   *Lope* (Gabon, W) First long-term study of sympatric chimpanzee and gorilla, in national park with own railway stop en route from coast (Libreville) to interior (Franceville). Most comfortable facilities of all, sited on breezy knoll, surrounded by rain forest. Electricity,

running water, refrigeration, even air-conditioned lab. Best food and drink, to French standards, such as fresh Brittany oysters on Christmas Day. Research set ecological and methodological standards still adhered to elsewhere. Founders: Caroline Tutin and Michel Fernandez (**83**).

9   *Lui Kotale* (Dem. Rep. Congo, W) One of few long-term study-sites of bonobo *(Pan paniscus)*. Remote and accessible only on foot, in midst of vast Congo River basin. Infrastructure primitive, but twice-weekly portered deliveries of fresh produce. Unprotected area with illegal hunting rampant, though not of bonobos. Site flat and marshy with verdant vegetation and varied animal life, especially insects. Superior scientific site, multiple communities habituated through sustained effort by Barbara Fruth and Gottfried Hohmann (**100, 101**).

10   *Mahale* (Tanzania, W) Second-oldest chimpanzee study site, 55+ years old, based at Kyoto University. Japanese equivalent of Gombe, further south on eastern shore of Lake Tanganyika, but more remote. In much bigger national park, accessible only by boat or sea-plane. Real mountains, up to 2460 metres elevation (Mt Nkungwe). Multiple groups under study, from woodland savanna to evergreen forest. Excellent fresh fish to eat from the lake. Founded by Toshisada Nishida (**85, 86, 99**). (Fig. 20)

11   *Ngogo* (Uganda) Neighbouring site to Kanyawara, in Kibale National Park, only a few kilometres apart. Shared links to two major American universities (Michigan, Yale), so steady stream of top-rank researchers. Home to biggest community (by far!) of chimpanzees, numbering

more than 200, but now splitting into two. Good infrastructure, including cold beer, easy access to Fort Portal. Directed by John Mitani and David Watts.

12 *Nimba* (Guinea) Highest mountains in West Africa, straddling borders of Guinea, Ivory Coast, and Liberia. Primitive camp requiring real commitment, especially with daily visits by countless honey bees, seeking moisture, which includes sweat. Stings daily! Slopes are steepest, often requiring four limbs instead of two to traverse. Chimpanzees do unusual things, such as eating freshwater crabs and butchering cannon-ball-sized fruit with stone tools. Hard work! Directed by Kathelijne Koops.

13 *Toro-Semliki* (Uganda, W) Protected area in far western Uganda, near border with Democratic Republic of Congo. Most diverse range of vegetation types, from arid scrub to evergreen forest to year-round swamps. Equally wide range of mammals, including elephant. Presence of poaching requires that researchers be accompanied by an armed ranger. Only customary well-digging population of wild chimpanzees. Best accommodation: Tents on breezy, raised wooden platforms. Directed by Kevin Hunt.

I have not worked at all the big sites, by a long shot, having missed out on Budongo (Uganda), Goualougo (Rep. of Congo), and Tai (Ivory Coast), among others. Forty years just was not long enough!

74 HABITUATION

Wild chimpanzees are initially wary of researchers, and rightly so. Their previous contacts with human beings may have been painful or even fatal. Chimpanzees are hunted or snared for bushmeat and maimed or killed for their crop-raiding, and it is humans who cut down the apes' forest homes that supply their food and shelter. Regrettably, uncaring humans, even careless researchers, may transmit deadly diseases to the wild apes, without knowing it. No wonder researchers find it frustrating to try to gather close-range behavioural data from their elusive wild subjects.

The solution is to *habituate* them, that is, to persuade the apes that these particular humans are not to be feared but instead can be tolerated, thus allowing observers close enough to record the details of their behaviour. Fully habituated chimpanzees allow familiar humans to follow them close-up, 5-10 metres away. An all-day follow from their arising in the morning to bedding down in the evening constitutes an equatorial 12-hour working day. A simple measure of full habituation is when a lone ape on the ground will go to sleep with a human close by, that is, with total trust. Early field workers accelerated habituation by *provisioning*, which is to provide irresistible food-items in association with themselves. Typically, a clearing in the forest would be stocked with bananas or sugar cane, and over time, the chimpanzees could be tempted to put up with humans at closer and closer distances as they came to chow down. This produced quick results, but it also caused problems that distorted the ape's behaviour, such as increased aggressive competition over prized foodstuffs.

Later researchers declined to provision and instead adopted an alternative strategy. They patiently presented themselves repeatedly to the apes until the apes finally realised that these humans were harmless. This technique may take years of rebuffing from the dubious apes before they acquiesce. In the early days at Fongoli, Susanna Johnson and I were once so frustrated that we tried singing to the chimpanzees, again and again, "You Are My Sunshine". They did linger longer that day, perhaps bemused by our strange behaviour. Happily, for any given study population, habituation only needs to be done once, as when established it becomes the norm. At Gombe, after 60+ years of study, the chimpanzees accept humans at close range as a mundane aspect in daily life.

Habituation for research has both positive and negative effects that go beyond the targeted chimpanzees, so now some researchers refuse to employ it. Other species may be habituated too, unintentionally. Baboons may turn up at a provisioning site to compete for the food, which may make their infants vulnerable to chimpanzee predation. 'Enlightened' or 'corrupted' baboons may learn to like human foods, which may lead to their raiding refuse facilities, or even waylaying people with food in hand. Refuse dumps may attract rodents, which then attract predatory, dangerous snakes.

Even if no feeding takes place and researchers are careful with rubbish, unanticipated effects may emerge. At Mahale, sympatric ungulates ranging from tiny blue duikers to medium-sized bushbucks tamed themselves, that is, they gradually became more and more comfortable at closer and closer distances to humans, grazing and browsing without fear. At Assirik, a flock of stone partridges, a wild species but resembling bantam chickens, became so nonchalant in foraging around camp that researchers had to take care not to stumble over them. Such inadvertent habituation seems puzzling, but it may be that the animals benefit from a research camp and its close environs being a sort of accidental 'predator-free zone', where they can relax.

75 CIRCUMSTANTIAL EVIDENCE

Studying unhabituated chimpanzees poses challenges to the field worker of the Sherlock Holmes variety, that is, inferring evidence of behaviour in the absence of the perpetrator. This task means first recognising that the material found *is* evidence and then inferring what is it evidence *of*. The first task is aided by associated signs of chimpanzee presence, which can be prints (hand, foot, knuckle, finger), ideally in soft soil; hair; faeces; wadges of chewed vegetation; and ultimately, DNA. The more of this associated evidence, the better! The second task is trickier, especially if the inferred activity is new to science. Having previously studied habituated chimpanzees is a great help, so that one already has many potential associations in mind. I was lucky to start chasing chimpanzees at Gombe, where habituation was total, before tackling unhabituated ones elsewhere.

The most obvious and useful evidence is the bed/nest, which shows undeniably that an ape was in that place. Even the oldest bed, leafless and falling to pieces, is a data-point reflecting the ranging of the local population. Also straightforward are signs of well-known extractive technology, such as the discarded tools used for termite fishing, ant dipping and nut cracking. Less useful are signs of basic feeding, especially on plant-parts that also are eaten by similarly large-bodied, sympatric primates, such as baboon or gorilla. For example, both chimpanzees and baboons eat the contents of the hard-shelled spherical fruit of *Strychnos*. Luckily for us, while baboons gain access to the contents by using their teeth, chimpanzees smash the fruits against rocks, using anvil percussion to crack open the shell. So, when we found abundant feeding remains at Issa, tooth-marked shells told us that the consumers were baboons, not chimpanzees. Just as for Holmes, interpretation is always a matter of probability, with the investigator hoping to increase the likelihood of accuracy with each new datum (Fig. 24).

Sometimes a field worker is stymied by being the first to encounter a phenomenon in the chimpanzee species' repertoire; here are some examples that mystified us at the outset, but were solved by later research findings:

- At Assirik, when tracking chimpanzees, we sometimes followed them to shallow pools in the laterite plateaux, where there were many splashes around the pool's edges. We supposed that for some unknown reason they were messy drinkers. Later work by Jill Pruetz at the nearby savanna site of Fongoli showed that chimpanzees there use such pools for bathing and resting, even engaging in watery leisure activities such as grooming and play.

- At Assirik, we also once found manufactured stick tools at the base of a dead tree. Scrutiny via binoculars showed a tree-hole high up in the trunk, which could have meant probing for honey, but none of the tools bore honey traces, and there was no sign of bees. Later, Pruetz and Bertolani showed that Fongoli chimpanzees were expert at making and using stick skewers to roust and disable bushbabies from their cavity homes.

- At Belinga, in Gabon, we found termite fishing probes, slender and flexible, at termite mounds, but with them were stouter, more rigid sticks, the function of which was a mystery. Luckily, we published a photo of these two types, which later were found by Crickette Sanz and David Morgan to be standard components of the advanced tool set used the Goualougo chimpanzees of Republic of Congo. The stouter tools turned out to be penetrative, puncturing 'drills' to access chambers of termites below the ground, which were then fished.

- At Assirik, a surprising case of extractive feeding without tools. Chimpanzees there eat the mesocarp contained in huge, rugby-ball-sized fruits of baobab trees. When the fruits are ripe, the rock-hard seeds pass intact through the gut of the ape and so appear intact in their faeces. We also found chewed-up seeds and smeared faeces on the sides of the buttress roots of the tree, with accompanying fingerprints, where the seeds had been picked out from the smelly matrix. Apparently, digestive passage through the gut of the apes had softened the seed coats, making the seeds' kernels available for re-cycled consumption. This was confirmed behaviourally at Fongoli.

- At savanna sites, watercourses dry up over the long dry season, so that eventually no surface water remains. Various animals from elephants to warthogs then dig 'wells' in the streambeds, to get access to drinking water. So it was at Assirik, but we never found enough digging by any species to tie digging technique or well characteristics to any of them. We suspected that chimpanzees might be digging such wells, but they could have been using the wells dug by other species. Only years later, in field work with Kevin Hunt at Semliki, could wells be tied to apes, for the chimpanzees there often dug in moist sandbars, presumably for easy digging without tools, leaving tell-tale finger-prints. Also, after digging a well, they used 'leaf-sponges' as absorbent tools, to get water from the wells without also getting a mouthful of sand. (Fig. 19)

One of the many attractions of primatological field work is such sleuthing!

Bertolani P & Pruetz JD (2011) Seed reingestion in savannah chimpanzees (*Pan troglodytes verus*) at Fongoli, Senegal. *International Journal of Primatology* 32: 1123-1132.

McGrew WC, Marchant LF & Hunt KD (2007) Ethoarchaeology of manual laterality: Well-digging by chimpanzees. *Folia Primatologica* 78: 240-244.

McGrew WC & Rogers ME (1983) Chimpanzees, tools and termites: New records from Gabon. *American Journal of Primatology* 5: 171-174.

Pruetz JD & Bertolani P (2007) Savannah chimpanzees, *Pan troglodytes verus*, hunt with tools. *Current Biology* 17: 412-417.

Sanz CM & Morgan DB (2007) Chimpanzee tool technology in the Goualougo Triangle, Republic of Congo. *Journal of Human Evolution* 52: 420-433.

76 TRANSECTION

"Transect: A line or strip across the earth's surface, along which a survey is made…along which a series of observations or measurements is made." (*Oxford English Dictionary*)

Simple but essential, transecting is the usual starting point of any ecological study, if only to characterise the environment in which research is to be done. Field primatologists use the method to study the abundance and distribution of any component of any place. It could be vegetation or resources or landmarks, fauna or flora, terrestrial or arboreal, or the primates themselves or their products. For unbiased, reliable data, strict rules of sampling and recording must apply; there is nothing so basic as a straight line cutting right through a space.

How to do a transect? It requires a team of people to cut, measure and record. The 'Cutter' clears the way ahead, as the line unfolds. 'Spotter' looks for presence of the targets and when found, measures them. 'Recorder' notes the distances travelled and details of the targets, such as location, dimensions, etc. The straight line must be maintained without deviation; if you come to a stream, it must be crossed, if a cliff, it must be climbed. Once, at Mahale, the line led to a cottage, through which we walked, in the front door and out the back. Transecting requires concentration and can be exhausting, especially on slopes, but once a rhythm is established, it can be a satisfying routine, with guaranteed data.

Anthony Collins and I did major transecting in Tanzania in 1982-83: We sought to compare the habitats of three groups of chimpanzees in two national parks on the eastern side of Lake Tanganyika, Gombe and Mahale. The two parks are bounded on the west by the lake and on the east by the escarpment of the great Albertine Rift, which slashes through East Africa, the result of tectonic plates moving apart. We did almost 16 km of transects (a modest amount by today's standards!), each from the lake shore upwards to the steep slopes of the upper scarp.

We recorded vegetation (six types from trees to herbs) and topography (altitude, slope, aspect, substrate). The results showed variation across sites, but the mosaic combination of forest and woodland resembled that envisioned for our hominoid ancestors who lived in the Miocene period, millions of years ago. It remains the most detailed and comprehensive ecological study of wild chimpanzee habitats, but the environment was only the background data for a more specific study of chimpanzee diet.

Chimpanzees everywhere in Africa are faunivores, that is, they eat animals, and some of their most important prey are social insects, that is, ants, bees and termites. The termites are perhaps the most interesting, for their acquisition involves elementary technology, that is, making and using tools to extract the prey from their earthen mounds. We were interested in what species of termites they chose from the wide range available and which ones required tool-assisted harvesting. We recorded frequency and distribution of mounds in relation to environmental variables. We found that the chimpanzees ate more than one kind but not the most common one; instead, they concentrated on the termites with the biggest body-size, although they were more uncommon.

In censusing, transects are done to collect data on direct encounters with chimpanzees, either by sight or sound, or if the apes are wary, one can record indirect data based on the products of their behaviour, especially their beds. As each individual builds a new one every night, this approximate one-to-one ratio indicates local population size, at least when based on fresh nests, made just the night before.

You may wonder why such basic methods are still needed in these days of precise, high-powered satellite imagery and drones. Why not just count trees or mounds or nests from above? Such data still require 'ground-truth' validation, at least at the outset of a study, and even then, transect data collection may be necessary in multi-layered, evergreen tropical vegetation. Transects still need doing!

Collins DA & McGrew WC (1988) Habitats of three groups of chimpanzees (*Pan troglodytes*) in western Tanzania compared. *Journal of Human Evolution* 17: 553-574.

Collins DA & McGrew WC (1987) Termite fauna related to differences in tool-use between groups of chimpanzees (*Pan troglodytes*). *Primates* 28: 457-471.

77 SHIT HAPPENS

Frankly, most people don't like to think about, much less handle, faeces. But these excretions can be very important to primatologists, even if dealing with them takes some getting used to. Actually, being primarily fruit-eaters, chimpanzee faeces can be surprisingly sweet-smelling; it is carnivore faeces that are hard to stomach! Dung, scats, stools, etc., whatever you call them, are ubiquitous in apes; defecation happens daily, sometimes several times, is easily detected, often by odour, and all do it, thereby gifting data to the world in a convenient, concentrated package. Apes do not defecate randomly in time or space. Knowing this, primatologists most easily find these packets of data by focusing on last night's nest site. Like humans, apes often start their day by defecation, so the easiest way to collect samples (before the dung beetles steal it) is the next morning, the sooner the better.

Consider *diet*. How to know what chimpanzees eat, if they are too elusive to be observed? (see **74**) Feeding remains may help, but only probabilistically until confirmed by direct observation, especially if a study site contains several primate species living sympatrically. What goes in one end must come out the other! Anything that is indigestible in the ape gut, such as bone, tooth, feather, scale, nail, etc., of vertebrates, and chitinous exoskeleton, shell fragments, opercula, etc. of invertebrates, persists. Even otherwise mushy caterpillars have indigestible mouthparts. All provide evidence of faunivory. Similarly for plants, some parts are readily identifiable, especially seeds, some of which even are evolved to survive passage through the consumer's gut in order to be dispersed, contributing to the plant's reproductive success. So, herbivory is detectable too.

More than food remnants emerge in faeces. Intestinal parasites, especially worms, have their eggs or larvae expelled out into the world, to infect other organisms. Rarely, even intact adult worms are passed. These stowaways provide data on their host's health and condition. Evidence of consumption of soil (*geophagy*)) may also survive gut passage. All of the above, and more, can be found by sluicing water and faeces through a sieve with 1mm mesh. Primatologists have used macroscopic techniques for decades at the early stages of fieldwork, if the apes are hard to find. Before Jane Goodall became famous, she did her share. (Fig. 13)

Nowadays, microscopic and molecular techniques provide far more information about all sorts of things. Much of what is cited here comes from the world's expert, Caroline Phillips. For example, the soft tissues of plants contain *phytoliths* (literally 'plant-stones'), microscopic, crystal-like secretions of specific plant tissues that enable identification of their sources, even to species. Stable *isotopes* of carbon and nitrogen reveal diet at the elemental level. Evidence even persists in fossilised faeces (*coprolites*), thus allowing comparison between extant and extinct apes or humans. (Fig. 21)

The trump card is DNA, as it too can be recovered from these smelly sources, so the precise make-up of dietary intake is genomically clear, via high-throughput sequencing. Faeces also contain information about the consumer, via shed epithelial cells from its gut walls. Chromosomes enable identification of sex, male or female. Genotyping reveals parentage and relatives, and most important, individual identification. Thus, a primatologist can know the size, sex ratio, kinship, composition, etc., that is, demography, of a chimpanzee community without ever setting eyes on them. Combined with other sources of DNA, such as saliva from discarded termite fishing tools, one can determine who was doing what extractive foraging and how at a particular place and time.

Yes, shit happens, thank goodness!

McGrew WC, Marchant LF, Phillips CA (2009) Standardised protocol for faecal analysis. *Primates* 50: 363-366.

Phillips CA, Wrangham RW, McGrew WC (2017) Non-dietary analytical features of chimpanzee scats. *Primates* 58: 393-402.

78 GIMME SHELTER

The Rolling Stones' plea applies more generally, as it reflects the widespread assumption that the bare minimum requirements for all animals' survival are water, food and shelter. The first one is obvious, the second varies greatly, but the third is more complicated, dependent on definition. Popular opinion may focus on 'a roof right over our heads', *a la* Bob Marley, but defined as 'a buffer, usually a barrier, to the thermoregulatory challenges of the elements, usually weather or climate', makes more inclusive sense. Important differences exist: A hermit crab prizes its home in an empty gastropod shell, while naked mole rats construct an underground abode. The crab *uses* a found object, while mole rats *make* their burrowed shelter.

Among primates, the great apes are the experts at constructing shelters, although countless bird species put them in the shade, so to speak. Every individual bonobo, chimpanzee, gorilla, and orangutan past the age of weaning builds at least one shelter per day for the rest of its life. Before then, in infancy and early childhood, it sleeps in the construction of its mother, from whom it learns the necessary techniques. It must do, because after the birth of her next offspring, it is turfed out, to build its own satellite structure nearby, until it achieves full independence.

Primatologists label these great ape shelters made of vegetation with various names: bed, nest, sleeping platform, etc. (Fig. 1) This lack of consensus in terminology reflects differing aspects, based on the structure's features: Its typically cup-like shape *resembles* the simple nests of most passerine birds. It *functions* as a comfortable mattress on which to recline and rest. It is *constructed* usually of and in woody vegetation, sometimes tens of metres up in the canopy.

Each of these labels is somehow problematic. Birds' *nests* are principally places for reproduction, to lay and incubate eggs, then to house immature, flightless youngsters until fledging. Apes use their shelters in this way only twice, at birth and (if lucky) at death. Skeletons have been found in them! *Bed* suggests a movable, reusable object, minimally a futon, but for apes they are fixed and immobile, mostly used for one night only, unless the maker is temporarily incapacitated by illness. *Platform* suggests elevation, but in addition to obligatory overnight nests, apes often make daytime nests on the ground, especially in the wet season, for napping. For the sake of convenience only, the simplest term, bed, is used here.

To what extent are these constructions architectural? How complex and variable are the products of bedmaking? How much and in what ways do they vary, serving multiple functions? How long do they last? These questions and many others have been tackled in chimpanzees principally by four researchers: Adriana Hernandez-Aguilar, Kathelijne Koops, David Sampson, and Fiona Stewart. Happily for me, I collaborated with each of them, in one way or another. Adriana focused on the detailed and multivariate environmental aspects of bedmaking, on a landscape scale, that is, basically the broadest ecology of bed-use. Kathelijne tested a variety of selection pressures, such as response to predation, insect vectors of disease, weather variables such as wind flow, etc, and compared arboreal *versus* terrestrial beds. David scrutinised the structure of nests, by deconstructing them into their components of bough, branch, twig, leaf, etc. I was below the tree when he first detached a whole, intact bed and dropped it to the ground, to be taken carefully to pieces. Fiona also looked at potential natural selection pressures, using participant observation, such as sleeping overnight in chimpanzee beds, with thermocouples attached to measure her skin temperature when exposed to the elements or buffered by the bed. (Fig. 29)

Bedmaking is universal across the great apes, but is it uniform, within or across species? The latter is unlikely for simple anatomical reasons, such as the greater body-size of gorillas inclining them to sleep on the ground, rather than risking falls from the canopy. Within-species variation is more promising to explore. Decades ago we published the first comparative study of chimpanzee nests, based on data from rainforest in Rio Muni (now Equatorial Guinea) and from savanna in Senegal. Many differences emerged between the two populations, but all of them may have reflected environmental differences between the two sites. Chimpanzees bed down at lower heights in savanna than in rainforest, reflecting the higher heights of trees in the forest.

Given that other forms of chimpanzee elementary technology show *cultural* variation across populations, what about bedmaking? No one yet has focused study on this question. The seminal source for chimpanzee cultural variation compared 39 types of behaviour for six populations of chimpanzees across Africa. Only one type, pillow-making, concerns beds. Study of bedmaking behaviour is made difficult by its taking place mostly up in the trees, rather than on the ground. Camera traps are unlikely to be a solution. Even if they can be mounted up in the canopy, how to choose the site, as chimpanzees are nomadic in choosing where to sleep. Perhaps drones are the answer? The question of whether or not chimpanzee bedmaking is cultural remains an enduring challenge.

Baldwin PJ, Sabater Pi J, McGrew WC & Tutin CEGT (1981) Comparison of nests made by different populations of chimpanzees (*Pan troglodytes*). *Primates* 22: 474-486.

McGrew WC (2021) Sheltering chimpanzees. *Primates* 62: 445-455.

79 REAL-LIFE ALTRUISM

An altruist does something that benefits another but incurs a personal cost in doing so. Thus, it is not so common in daily life, especially if the potential cost is great. Here is my best example. Once I was en route home to Scotland after a field season in Senegal. I was cutting it close, trying to squeeze every day out of my precious field time, so I travelled straight from the bush to Dakar airport at the last minute. The airline had assured me that my ticket would be waiting at the check-in desk. However, having got to the front of the check-in queue, I was told that no such ticket was there. Instead, I'd have to go into the city to the airline's office to pick it up, but in doing so, of course, I would miss my booked flight. I despaired, as there might not be a seat available for some days, and I was due to resume teaching immediately upon getting back home at the University of Stirling.

Then, the man in the queue behind me, a complete stranger, enquired about the problem. I explained, and he offered to buy me a ticket on the spot! I was so astonished that at first I could not believe him. He said he would use his credit card to do so, and that I could just mail him a cheque in repayment, once I got home. What a chance he was taking, as a ticket from Dakar to London to Edinburgh cost several hundred pounds! I accepted gratefully, made my flight, and got home in time. I sent him the cheque shortly thereafter. He was an American missionary, but of course I didn't get to know him during this brief but crucial encounter. Perhaps he was just a good guy.

Occasionally, being altruistic unexpectedly pays off. Here is a trivial example from years later: Once, while standing in a queue at the bar in a crowded Cambridge pub, the Fort St George, I heard a man say that he that he was 50 pence short of paying for the round of drinks that he'd just got. He was distressed, as the pressure from all the others waiting to order their drinks was obvious. So, I just gave him a 50 pence coin. He accepted, paid up, and left, carrying his tray of drinks, saying that he would find me later. Indeed, he did, but it was a nice bottle of wine that he handed over, not 50 pence! Altruism rewarded!

Was there any connection between the two events? Perhaps there's something about queueing, or is it just the proverbial kindness of strangers?

80 FIELD HAZARDS

When people think of hazardous animals in the wilds of Africa, they mostly focus on big herbivores, such as elephant or rhinoceros, or big carnivores, such as lion or leopard. Or they call to mind dangerous reptiles, such as venomous snakes or crocodiles. However, much smaller, inconspicuous creatures also present threats to health (see **81**).

Mostly these pests are disease vectors, such as mosquitoes carrying malaria, or tsetse flies carrying sleeping sickness. Also debilitating but invisible are endo-parasites, which accordingly are harder to detect.

Once, shortly after returning to Stirling from Senegal, I had symptoms of tummy upset. At first, I thought it was indigestion, but it persisted, no matter what I ate. Perhaps it was an ulcer? Then, one day I looked into the toilet bowl and saw in my faeces what looked like the remains of a pasta dinner. I'd not been eating pasta, or anything that resembled it. When I looked closer, I saw that the white shiny fragments were not pasta, but the shed proglottids from an adult tapeworm affixed in my gut. I recognised this unwelcome resident decades after studying invertebrate taxonomy as an undergraduate zoology major.

I fished out a few, preserved them in alcohol, and took the vial along to my GP in Bridge of Allan. I handed them to Dr Richard Simpson without explanation. He was puzzled for a second or two, then his face lit up. He exclaimed, with surprising enthusiasm, "I've not seen these since medical school!" After getting over the delight at encountering something unusual in his daily routine of patients, he prescribed the necessary medication to void my gut of my parasitical passenger. Relief followed, after 24 hours of spending time close to the toilet.

A question remained: How had I acquired it? Our diet at the Assirik field camp included almost no fresh meat, so not there. Tapeworms are acquired only by eating raw or minimally cooked flesh in which their larvae are encysted. Then, it dawned on me. Very occasionally, we took a break at the Simenti tourist lodge, run by a couple of French guys, Michel Fernandez and Patrice Marty, at the other end of the park. Being French, they served their local beef rare, and presumably this meant that the steak I'd eaten with such pleasure had not been cooked right through. I suspect that other unsuspecting tourists took home similar stowaways, only to puzzle later how they acquired them!

81 UNWELCOME COMPANIONS

Part of doing field work in the tropics is dealing with parasites, both internal (endo-) and external (ecto-). Neither is pleasant…

Coming back from a short stay in Costa Rican rain forest, I had some pinkish swellings on my legs. They seemed likely to be insect bites, as there were plenty of blood-sucking insects there, such as mosquitoes and ticks. Instead of fading away, the swellings grew in size. Scrutiny revealed that something alive was inside the muscle tissue, just below the skin. Research online showed them to be the larvae of bot flies, the adults of which lay eggs on other insects, which in turn pass them on to humans or other mammals. The larvae burrow into the host to complete their life cycle, finally to emerge as adult flies. Unless you feel inclined to be grossed out, I do not recommend going to YouTube with this, for you will find graphic footage of these events.

So, what to do? The simplest thing is just to let the life history unfold, then wave goodbye to the adult fly as it departs. They are not vectors of any disease and do no lasting harm to the host. It is a weird feeling to be nurturing such uninvited lodgers, so the obvious urge is to extract them, but the larvae are cunningly equipped to resist being dislodged, having erectile spines. Attempted extraction, especially by amateurs, can lead to infection. I tried extraction but failed and gave up, probably having killed them at an early stage, still embedded. My body then absorbed the remains and I lived happily ever after.

How had I acquired them? It probably came via clothing hanging outdoors in the open to dry, on which insects had laid eggs. The laundry should have been hung inside a screened-in porch.

A similar infestation occurred in Uganda, in Kibale National Park, at the Kanyawara field site, via another type of insect, the mango fly. Linda Marchant and I arrived late at Richard Wrangham's house, and after one of his assistants made up the bed, we retired. Richard arrived even later. The next morning, Richard and I awoke with our heads and necks speckled in irritating, red spots, but somehow Linda had escaped. These spots indicated the location of mango fly larvae that had hatched and burrowed in under the skin. The simple, standard solution was to dab each spot with a drop of clear nail varnish. This treatment would cut off the air (oxygen) supply to the insect within, thus killing it, but no varnish was found in camp, which dictated a stop in Fort Portal, on the way to Entebbe. Richard was to present a scientific paper there later that day. Alas, the hoped-for source of nail varnish in town had no clear type, so we were forced to take shocking red. Thus, Richard had the choice of no treatment and increasing irritation or of having his face dotted with bright crimson spots. He bravely chose the latter and gave his paper.

How had this happened? The camp's normal routine to prevent such infestations was to hot-iron air- dried clothing, which would kill the eggs. Someone had neglected to iron some pillow covers, and Richard and I had used un-ironed ones, while Linda had been luckier!

82 FIGAN'S AND MY PREDICAMENT

One day at Gombe, I was doing a lone follow of Figan, a prime adult male chimpanzee, just him and me. Basically, I trailed along after him as he did his solitary foraging. He took me to Plum Tree Thicket, a large area of dense, woody, shrubbery vines, almost impassable. He took me through one of the chimpanzee-made passages, which amounted almost to tunnels in the thick vegetation, about a metre high and wide. He and I moved quadrupedally, with me on hands and knees. All went fine, until about halfway through the thicket, when we heard chimpanzees' long calls (pant-hoots) from behind us. Abruptly, he turned around to face me, alert to the vocalisations.

I inferred that he wanted to reverse his travel, to return to whence we had come, presumably to deal with what was happening back there. I was blocking his way. What to do? We looked at one another, face to face, just inches away. Then, spontaneously, without a sound or gesture, he scrunched over to one side of the tunnel, and I did the same to the other side. We carefully squeezed past one another. We then set off again, with me still trailing him, to exit from the passage's entrance. A brief incident, something we human beings do unconsciously, when on a pavement or in a lift, but for me, it was a trivial but telling case of mutual theory of mind in action, across species. Each of us inferred what the other needed and acted accordingly.

83 TROPICAL FRUITERY

One of the rewards of working in the tropics is getting to know tropical fruits *in situ*, such as passion fruit, mango, guava, etc. Not only are they cheap to buy but also often can be hand-picked. My favourite of all is mango, a juicy, sticky joy to eat by hand, but accessing them in the bush is not always straight- forward.

Gombe National Park, the site of Jane Goodall's long-running research centre, is on the eastern side of Lake Tanganyika, in western Tanzania. The shore once had fishing villages dotted along it, and as one approaches her camp by boat, giant old mango trees can be seen, scattered along the shoreline, remnants of past human occupation. Depending on the season, one might see them burgeoning with flowers or immature green fruits and imagine the feast to come when the fruits ripen. One newcomer park warden was heard to say that when the mango season arrived, he would deploy his rangers to harvest them for sale in the nearby town of Kigoma. As chimpanzee researchers, we could imagine what pleasure the frugivorous apes would take in consuming them. Both humans and apes were to be disappointed, as it turned out that the local olive baboons, with their robust gut enzymes adapted to overcoming the deterrent secondary compounds of the unripe fruit, would triumph. By the time the fruits would have been ripe, they'd all been eaten by the baboons!

Some of the local fruits were familiar but different. The small bananas used at Gombe to provision the chimpanzees were much sweeter than their bigger but bland counterparts sold in Western supermarkets. Many of us found a reason to visit the banana storage locker to have a snack. At Mahale, researchers planted citrus trees for their consumption; the lemons were large and thick-peeled but tasty. Eventually, their chimpanzee subjects of study tried them and agreed. At Belinga, one of the benefits of occupying a villa in the deserted mining camp was access to remnant fruit trees. In our villa's back yard was a fine avocado tree, and the previous occupants even had left behind a snaring pole for pulling them down. For anyone like me who is an avocado-lover, it was heaven to have an unlimited supply on your doorstep.

The strangest case of fruitiness involved the humble tomato (which is a fruit!). In the wonderfully- appointed field camp at Lope, Michel Fernandez's design included a kitchen sink with running water. Its drain-pipe ran downslope until its end tens of metres distance away. Sometime after installation of this convenience, sounds of elephants were heard close by in the night. What was going on? Investigation during the day revealed a huge tomato patch, grown from seeds washed down the drain, which had been discovered by the elephants from the nearby forest. So, two large-brained mammals shared in harvesting the accidental bounty, one diurnally and one nocturnally.

What about wild fruits? I vowed early on in my chimpanzee chasing to sample every food-item that the chimpanzees ate, following the example of my friend, Toshisada Nishida. I kept to this resolution, except for their primate prey. Thus, I ate many fruits of many plants, woody and otherwise, from trees, shrubs, lianas, etc. Most were not notable, often being tough, bland, or fibrous, compared with the sugary-selected mainstays of temporal climates, such as apple, pear, plum, etc.

Some were downright unpleasant, such as those with latex sap, but others were delicious. If asked to name a favourite, it would be the grape-sized fruits of hog plum. Tart but also sweet, juicy, and delicious even when just slightly fermented. The chimpanzees at Assirik favoured them too, and as the trees sometimes grew in bountiful groves, they could support many ape consumers at once, with the scene echoing with food calls. So profuse was the fruiting that uneaten fruit decaying on the ground produced plumes of irresistible, ethanolic scent, detectable on the breeze from tens of metres away.

84 JOB-HUNTING

My first permanent, tenure-track job in academia unexpectedly was handed to me on a platter. My post-doc from Stanford was finishing, and I wanted to get back to Scotland, but I was then in the field, in East Africa. More precisely, I was at Gombe, in far western Tanzania, chasing Jane Goodall's wild chimpanzees. In those pre-internet days, my sole source of information in the bush about current job vacancies back in the UK was the *Guardian Weekly*, a digest of the best stories in that UK newspaper, printed on tissue-thin paper, sent by air mail. I scanned the classified adverts and posted off applications for lectureships going in Scotland or northern England.

This effort proved to be discouraging. Some universities never replied, probably rightly figuring that if they could not pay travel expenses to attend an interview, then a poor post-doc was even less likely to do so. As time went on, I became desperate enough to offer to pay my own travel expenses, but that didn't help. Some sent back polite rejections.

One was more enterprising: St Andrews University supplied a phone number in the nearby town of Kigoma, offering me a telephone interview at an appointed time on an appointed date. Unfortunately, the invitation letter arrived after that date, so I stood them up without even knowing it. As I write this now, I'm an Honorary Professor at St Andrews, 45 years later, but presumably no one is still around at the university to recall my missed interview in 1973.

Then, the University of Stirling offered me a job based solely on my application and letters of reference! Without an interview! How could this be? Stirling was a young and under-financed university, then at the lowest rung on the academic totem-pole, but they normally interviewed applicants just like any other university. I was later to learn that I'd benefited from an improbable confluence: Four members of staff in the Psychology Dept. at Stirling had been colleagues of mine at earlier stages of our careers: Richard Bambridge, Cliff Henty, and Philip Smith at Oxford, and Robin Campbell at Edinburgh. Apparently they'd formed a delegation and persuaded the Head of Department, Peter McEwen, to take me on. Decades later, I remain grateful for their vouching for me, but I do not recommend that any job-seeker rely on such rare good fortune!

P.S. My starting salary in 1973 at Stirling as a Lecturer was a princely 3300 pounds.

85 SCHEHERAZADE THE HEN

While being hosted at Mahale by Professor Junichiro Itani, Caroline Tutin and I spent a week at an outlying camp, Myako, which had been 'mothballed' but was utterly charming, if a bit remote. To make life more pleasant, he generously sent us a hen on the second day, to provide us with a chicken dinner. She arrived, trussed up and clucking, but too late in the day for supper preparations. When we checked on her the next morning, in her tiny, crude cage, she had laid an egg! This was a delightful surprise, so we ate the egg for breakfast. It was so tasty that we made a deal with her that so long as she laid an egg every day, she would be spared the chop. So she did, until it was time to return to the main camp at Kansyana. Back she came with us, to rejoin her colleagues in the flock there, no worse for her travels. Prof. Itani was a bit surprised but seemed to understand our arrangement. (Fig. 6)

86 CUSTOMARY GROOMING

All primates groom. They use their hands and mouths to clean body surfaces, either their own or others (see **44**). This activity makes up a surprisingly high proportion of their daily lives, far exceeding the amount needed for bodily hygiene. Such reciprocal servicing creates bonding, from the earliest grooming received by infants from their mothers to prolonged exchanges between doddery elders. Such universality suggests uniformity, but at least for chimpanzees, the situation is more varied.

Caroline Tutin and I realised this when we first visited the Japanese field site in the Mahale Mountains, hosted by Prof. Junichiro Itani. On our first day in the forest, we saw a variant of social grooming that had not been recorded at Gombe, which is close by in Tanzania. Even after 14 years of observation of Gombe's chimpanzees, Jane Goodall had not seen the behavioural pattern that we called the 'grooming hand-clasp' (GHC). (Fig. 25)

The GHC's postural configuration is striking: Two adult chimpanzees sit facing one another, and each raises vertically either the left or right hand, to full extension overhead. Those two hands are clasped, maintaining the posture, while each of the other (free) hands engage in mutual grooming of the revealed armpit of the grooming partner. A striking and symmetrical bodily configuration, resembling an A-frame! We were astonished, and later, at the end of the day, we asked Prof. Itani about it. He was surprised at our interest, saying he assumed that all chimpanzees did this.

This simple but clear behavioural difference between two Tanzanian populations of chimpanzees suggested variation in *customs* between groups, or the presence of *culture*, a trait then assumed to be uniquely human. Unlike other kinds of chimpanzee variation, for example in foraging technology, which might simply reflect environmental influence, GHC was purely social, unrelated to ecological variables. Nor was it likely to be genetically determined, as the Gombe and Mahale populations likely evolved from the same founding stock on the eastern shore of Lake Tanganyika. So, naively, we sent off a descriptive manuscript for publication, to the most prestigious journal in British anthropology, *Man* (later re-named *Journal of the Royal Anthropological Institute*). Luckily for us, the editor, Peter Loizos, was generous and far-sighted, recognising that, although about apes, it had resonance for socio-cultural anthropology, so our report was published.

Since then, GHC has turned up in several populations

of chimpanzees across Africa, and with further nuanced variation, for example, the particular grips used in the GHC also vary, such as whether the fingers are interlaced or not. In populations in which snare-injury causes loss of a hand, such an individual still does GHC, with the partner grasping the other's stump. Other populations have yet to show it, including other long-term sites, such as Bossou and Tai, studied for decades. This inconsistency might suggest that GHC has been independently invented within populations, on multiple occasions, but that without such innovation, it remains unexpressed. On the other hand, it could have been invented just once in a region, then defused to neighbouring communities of the apes, via emigration. One way to study the latter is to follow the normal dispersal of females from their natal communities to the one in which they will live thereafter. Do the immigrant females maintain the GHC version of their upbringing or do they change it to conform to the version of GHC that they find in their new community? Some observations suggest that they can do either.

McGrew WC & Tutin CEG (1978) Evidence for a social custom in wild chimpanzees? *Man* 13: 234-251.

87 SAHARA CROSSING

In 1976, the Stirling African Primate Project (SAPP) began, when three of us drove from Scotland to Senegal, taking 42 days to travel 10,149 kilometres (6306 miles). Our vehicle (Jezebel) was a second-hand, 6-cylinder, petrol Land Rover, bought from a Stirlingshire farmer. The route took us through:

Scotland, England, France, Spain, Morocco, Algeria, Niger, Upper Volta, Mali, and Senegal. In those days, there were three possible North-South routes across the Sahara Desert: (1) *Coastal* from Morocco to Spanish Sahara to Mauretania to Senegal; (2) *Western* from Algeria directly to Mali, then Senegal; (3) *Eastern*, as described above. Coastal was first-choice, but civil war had recently broken out in Spanish Sahara, making the route dangerous. Western (through Timbuktu!) was straight-forward but we lacked the fuel capacity to make the longest leg across the middle of the desert. So, we took the longest, most indirect Eastern route.

Pamela Baldwin and I drove down from Stirling to London, to pick up Jon Pollock. (Fig. 8) She and I were 'newbies', but Jon had done the trans-Sahara journey once before. His experience, especially of vehicle repair, turned out to be critical, especially as the journey unfolded (see **88**). We crossed the Channel from Dover to Calais by hovercraft and made two stops in France before turning south. By the time we got to Barcelona, it was clear that Jezebel needed stronger rear springs, as the standard ones were suffering from an over-full load. We bought these from a Santana (Spanish equivalent of Land Rover) dealer and changed them on the beach, with help from a passing-by mechanic.

We crossed the Mediterranean by ferry from Algeciras to Cueta, a Spanish colonial enclave embedded in Morocco. From there on, we camped overnight, which meant daily unloading and re-loading tent, camp beds, etc. We drove east to Algeria before turning south, but the route across the desert was surfaced only halfway, to Tamanrasset. After that, it was just rock and sand, and for days we saw not a single living plant, except at rare oases. Camping out in January in the desert meant overnight sub-freezing temperatures, but during the day, it was pleasant sunshine. The unmarked track meant getting lost a few times and having to dig ourselves out of dunes (god bless sand ladders!). En route, we met everything from gerbils to a solitary Tuareg.

The rodents scurried around our camp beds as we tried to sleep, apparently looking for food scraps. One evening a man silently emerged from the darkness, wearing a very long sword. We were sitting around a campfire, having coffee, so we offered him some. He accepted but didn't stay long, then walked off back into the darkness. Was he navigating by the stars?

Eventually, we reached northern Niger, and that first cold beer after 15 'dry' days tasted wonderful. We then turned west, stopping at each capital city for visas to the next country (Niamey, Ouagadougou, Bamako). We had intended to veer north to follow the Niger River to Senegal but were told that fuel shortages along the way meant that we could not be guaranteed fill-ups. So, ever-optimistic and opportunistic, we drove the vehicle onto a flat-bed railway wagon, got securely cabled onto it, and rode the rails for four days to Tambacounda, in eastern Senegal. Flat-bed railway wagons are just bare platforms, lacking any amenities, such as toilets, but somehow we survived, mostly by dozing in the heat. Unloaded in Tamba, we had only to drive across Senegal to the coast, in order to do government paperwork that allowed us to start chasing chimpanzees in the Parc National du Niokolo-Koba, at Mont Assirik. Hence began SAPP.

88 GRAVITY RULES

Halfway across the Sahara, in southern Algeria, the fuel pump on our Land Rover, Jezebel, packed in, leaving the three of us stranded in the middle of nowhere (see **87**). Unlike other mechanical engine parts such as a carburettor that can be taken apart, mended and put back together, the fuel pump was a sealed electronic unit. A replacement was needed. So, what to do?

Before leaving, Pamela Baldwin and I had done the weekend Land Rover maintenance course for dummies at Solihull, but it had told us nothing that would help here. All we two could think of was to wait for the next vehicle to come along and then try to hitch a ride to the nearest town to try to get a new pump. We saw only a few vehicles each day and the nearest town was a long way away. Having driven the Sahara before, Jon knew that such tasks required lateral thinking…

He said that the sole function of the pump was to get the petrol from the tank to the carburettor, so why not let gravity do the work? That is, remove the auxiliary fuel tank from under the front seat and move it up onto the roof rack, then run a plastic hose directly from the tank to the carburettor below. Problem solved! Of course, this presented an obvious fire hazard, if the hose came loose and sprayed petrol everywhere, but we were desperate enough to risk this.

The transfer took a while to accomplish, but it got done. It was strange to be driving along, watching the petrol flowing down a plastic hose along the edge of the windscreen. We arrived safely in Niamey, Niger, found a new fuel pump, restored Jezebel to her original configuration, and continued on our way.

89 RE-WILD? RE-INTRODUCE? RELEASE? REHABILITATE!

We never planned to study western chimpanzees in West Africa, but when the Gombe kidnapping occurred in 1975, that planned-for option was closed. Rebels from Zaire crossed Lake Tanganyika to kidnap and hold hostage four students from Gombe, thus shutting down expatriate research there. Luckily for us, Stella Brewer then invited us to join her at Mt. Assirik, in the Parc National du Niokolo-Koba, in Senegal. She was rehabilitating a small group of ex-captive chimpanzees on one side of the mountain but said that there were plenty of wild chimpanzees in the area, so we set up camp on the other side of the mountain, a 30-minute drive away from her base. So began research in the Stirling African Primate Project (SAPP) in 1976.

Stella had a motley group of ape refugees, from very different backgrounds. Her goal was to enable as many as possible of them to adapt and thrive in a natural, chimpanzee-friendly habitat. Some of them had been wildborn in West Africa and had been confiscated by wildlife authorities and sent to the Abuko Nature Reserve, in neighbouring Gambia. They had been captured young and had survived hard times in captivity for various lengths of time before reaching Abuko, having never left West Africa. Others were young chimpanzees who had been kept as pets in Europe, home-reared by well-intentioned but naïve owners. Finally, some had been born in European zoos but for various reasons had not done well there. They had been donated (offloaded?) to Stella's project, which got the zoos off the hook but put her on it.

For the zoo chimpanzees, there was no 're-' entailed. They had no experience of life beyond a European cage, and to have turned them loose *de novo* in an intact ecosystem with a full complement of predators and competitors would have been fatal. Captive-born status for them meant total ignorance of survival skills. Instead, Stella had to try to inculcate these skills, acting as a human model, essentially being a surrogate mother. They had to learn to eat wild foods, which meant learning to forage on the right vegetation at the right time of year. Assirik is a highly seasonal environment, with a 7-month dry season, when even drinking water sometimes is scarce. They had to learn to sleep above the ground, for overnight terrestriality meant vulnerability to nocturnal predators, such as lion, leopard, spotted hyaena, etc. They had to learn to recognise and avoid hazards, especially venomous snakes, such as cobra, mamba, viper, etc. Wild-born and raised chimpanzees learn such skills from their mothers and siblings, but these 'newbies' were in a state of ignorance, burdened with a set of unsuitable habits. They had to be patiently rehabilitated, one step at a time.

Happily, Stella found a 'teaching assistant' in Tina, a pre-adolescent individual who must have had years of childhood experience in that type of habitat, for she quickly adapted to doing all the right things. She ended up teaching Stella about seasonal foods. She was an expert nest-builder and was savvy enough to spot and warn about hazards.

On another front, Nini and Bobo came as already-acquainted friends, through their human surrogate caregiver, Raffaella Savinelli, who came to hand them over but stayed on to help Stella. The real problems were the European zoo-reared individuals, who had never eaten natural food, etc. Why eat these fibrous, sometimes tasteless items from the bush, when you longed for grapes and apples? These individuals had to be weaned gradually from one diet to another. (Fig. 9)

What to do in the meantime? Stella was loath to put the apes back into cages, so she built a 'cage' for herself, a modest cottage of stone walls and corrugated metal roof with strong mesh window grilles. She built wooden sleeping platforms for the apes in nearby trees. Thus, the chimpanzees could live outside, free 24/7, while Stella was confined, especially, at meal-times. Daily, the resident humans and apes took long walks in the surrounding forest and woodlands, as the chimpanzees came to know the location and processing of the wild foods, especially fruits, as they came into season. Tina was a tremendous help in this acclimatisation, in the broadest sense.

Where did SAPP come in? In its first year, we spent much time in Stella's camp, also learning about chimpanzee diet, ranging, etc. We did spells of chimpanzee-sitting, often accompanying the two Senegalese assistants, Rene and Bruno, whom Stella had hired, when she had to be away. We helped with the rehabilitation when possible, for example, munching wild foods with gusto, and tempting them to do the same. We alternated with her on logistical chores, such as supply trips to Tambacounda, a five-hour drive away.

So, what went wrong? Why did Stella abandon the project and move the chimpanzees to an island in the Gambia River?

Plain and simple: the resident wild chimpanzees of the area resisted the presence of the intruders. Uneasy encounters in the bush led to increasing harassment by the locals, to the extent of their raiding Stella's camp. Chimpanzees are fiercely territorial and they were defending their resources. Rather than risk fatality to her charges, Stella took them to The Gambia, where their descendants live today, on islands in a national park.

SAPP was left on its own, which turned out to be important, as we later learned that the wild chimpanzees from the far side of Assirik had a huge home range, the largest known of any wild population. We confirmed this when we found one of 'our' adult males, Brown Bear, during a later survey on Stella's side of the mountain. So, with no little irony, our project's progress benefited from the departure of Stella's, which had enabled us to begin SAPP in the first place.

Brewer S (1978) *The Chimps of Mt. Asserik*. Alfred A Knopf, New York, 302 pp.

90 ASSIRIK DAILY LIFE

Chimpanzee field research is done in many places, and everyday life at those sites varies accordingly. Some of the variation is dictated by constraints of environment, funding, politics, personalities, etc. Some of it reflects personal preferences and experiences of the researchers, especially a project's leaders. Caroline Tutin and I shared this role in the Stirling African Primate Project, at Mt. Assirik, in the Parc National du Niokolo-Koba (PNNK), Republic of Senegal.

PNNK is a huge park, most of which is savanna, that is, grassland-dominated, with deciduous woodland. However, the Gambia River cuts through it, and its tributaries support ribbons of evergreen riverine forest, thus allowing chimpanzees to survive, even to thrive, in a hot, dry and open environment. (Fig. 7)

We did a four-year (1976-79) project there, seeking to the first ecological and ethological study of savanna-living chimpanzees. We based ourselves by one of the major watercourses descending from its source at the summit of Mt. Assirik, the highest point in the park. At the time, PNNK had a full complement of large herbivores and their predators: elephant, buffalo, eland, hartebeest, etc, plus lion, leopard, spotted hyena, African wild dog, etc. Faunally, Assirik was then unique among all chimpanzee study sites.

The park authorities stipulated that only researchers could reside in camp, that no permanent structures could be erected, and that only a handful of personnel could be resident at any one time. Thus, we had none of the usual local guides, trackers, cooks, domestic help, etc. that typically help field workers to do their work. It was the most basic of the many field sites I met in 40 years of chasing wild chimpanzees. By the same token, this minimal lifestyle also made it for me the most memorable and satisfying.

The camp was sited on the edge of a wide, impervious laterite pan. Up to five of us at a time lived in local- style huts of sapling frame, woven bamboo walls, and grass-thatched roof, with earthen floor. All materials came from on-site. Huts were mostly for sleeping and storage, and most daily life occurred outdoors, under a thatched canopy. The accommodation was simple but perfectly attuned to the local conditions. (Fig. 11)

Normally, we cooked over a campfire, on wood gathered daily. Eventually a stone oven got built for baking, a real luxury (see **94**). We had a camping gas back-up, for the depths of the rainy season, when firewood was sodden from rainfall or humidity. Drinking water came straight from a nearby stream, to be filtered only, with nothing else added, but it had to be carried up a steep slope from the stream, in 20-litre jerricans. We burned combustible rubbish, dispersed organic waste, but bagged inorganic, non-burnable waste, to take to park headquarters for disposal.

Personal hygiene normally meant bathing in the same stream, which also trebled up for laundry. The upstream-downstream gradient was drink-bathe-laundry. By the end of the dry season, bathing was limited to one bucket of water a day per person, as the stream dried up to almost nothing. However, in the rainy season, depressions in the laterite pan formed pools with running water, which created welcome bathing 'tubs'. The same ubiquitous sheet of laterite prevented digging a drop-toilet, so our excretions were broadcast, with each person having a 'territory'. The dung beetles took care of disposal.

We had no communication with the outside world, except when rare visitors dropped by and brought mail from park headquarters. We maintained a post-box for outgoing mail, so as to be ready to ask any visitors to take away mail for posting, but it rarely got emptied, given the rarity of visitors.

We had no electricity, so lighting was by kerosene lantern or candle. Similarly, there was no refrigeration, so most food was dry or tinned. Of course, on our infrequent supply trips (every 4-6 weeks) to the nearest town, Tambacounda, we brought back fresh food, but had to eat it quickly, before it went off in the heat.

All in all, a simple, challenging but somehow rewarding life!

McGrew WC, Baldwin PJ & Tutin CEG (1981) Chimpanzees in a hot, dry and open habitat: Mt. Assirik, Senegal, West Africa. *Journal of Human Evolution* 10: 227-244.

91 ASSIRIK CRITTERS

From Feb. 1976 to Dec. 1979, the Stirling African Primate Project did behavioural ecological fieldwork in the PNNK. To study western chimpanzee, Guinea baboon, green monkey and patas monkey, we based ourselves at Mt. Assirik, in the middle of one of the largest national parks in West Africa. Along the way, we encountered many other species, as Assirik had then the most intact and least disturbed fauna of any of the 140+ field sites in Africa where chimpanzees have been studied.

On our first night in the park, we bivouacked beside a stream, setting up camp beds around the campfire, to sleep under the stars, as it was dry season. Jon had gone to sleep and Pam and I had said our goodnights. Then, a flickery shadow passed between us and the fire, for a second or two, so fast that we could not be sure of what we'd seen. But when Pam and I conferred, in shaky voices, we agreed that it had been an adult lioness, strolling nonchalantly by, a couple of metres away.

What to do? We woke Jon, who grumbled and went back to sleep, having not really taken in what we were reporting. Or so he said the next morning. Pam did the sensible thing, which was to decamp to Jezebel, lock all her doors and rest secure. I took the nonsensical but somehow satisfying strategy of moving my camp bed into the tent. Of course, a lion easily could have slashed her way in, had she been inclined to do so!

This was not an isolated case. On another occasion, at our permanent camp, a visitor came to breakfast after his first night, saying that he'd met a lion en route, when walking from his hut to the dining area. He was completely calm, assuming that this sort of thing happened all the time.

Our favourite bathing spot was a temporary pool on the laterite plateau that filled up in the rainy season. It had trickles of inflow and outflow, making it ideal for those few months. There was a resident monitor lizard, which at the outset fled in alarm when we approached. With time, the reptile became more and more tolerant of the splashy strangers and remained unperturbed on his/her favourite perch, little more than a couple of metres away from the bather.

Other encounters were not so happy, at least for some. Great flocks of guinea fowl roamed through the grassland areas of the study site, and sometimes we met them when we were driving on our way home in the evenings. Then, for some inexplicable reason, the accelerator on the vehicle would jam at speed, such that an unlucky bird would end up as roadkill. What could we do then but retrieve and take the victim back to camp? You might be able to guess what we had for dinner that night.

Fishing was permitted in the park, and the little stream beside the camp had a few pools big enough to contain fish (see **4**). Given no access to fresh vertebrate protein, we sometimes used our days off work to go fishing, with simple hook and line. What to use as bait? It turned out that the fish were irresistibly attracted to tsetse flies. That is, they went for the flies with distended reddish abdomens that we had killed after they had sucked our blood. Each of us during out daily work kept a photographic film canister in our pocket to collect and accumulate these sanguinivores. Ah, sweet revenge!

McGrew WC, Baldwin PJ, Marchant LF, Pruetz JD, Tutin CEG (2014) Chimpanzees (*Pan troglodytes*) and their mammalian sympatriates: Mt. Assirik, Niokolo-Koba National Park, Senegal. *Primates* 55: 525-532.

92 AVIAN ENTERPRISE

As a zoologist, I somehow conceived the goal of publishing scientific journal articles on all the vertebrate classes, that is, mammal, bird, reptile, amphibian, and fish. As it turned out, 99% of mine were on mammals, and overwhelmingly, those papers were on primates. I did manage to publish short pieces on fishes, reptiles, and birds, but the last was pure serendipity.

Once at Assirik, I was walking back to camp via the bed of the little stream that was the watercourse of Lion Valley. In parts, the stream had almost cut a gorge through the laterite substrate, and in the resulting under-hang of the cliffs were the daytime roosting sites of large-bodied fruit bats. These are not the tiny 'flying mice' that are insect-eating bats, but the big fruit-eating ones of the tropics, the size of a winged rabbit. My arrival disturbed them, and some flew out in disarray. Suddenly, a bird of prey, later identified as a Gabar goshawk, swooped down and caught one of the bats in mid-air. The predator must have been sitting in one of the trees overhanging the stream. The struggling prey was so heavy that the two plummeted to ground and landed on the stream bank in a single, jumbled mass, only metres from my feet. I stood still, and either they didn't notice me or were too preoccupied to care. Then, the bird did something amazing. It dragged the bat to the water, and stood on it, with its wings outspread. The water's depth was only a few inches, but it was enough for the predator to submerge and drown the prey. Only after the bat ceased moving did the bird take wing and slowly and laboriously flew up to a nearby tree branch, loaded down with the prey in its talons. Then, it went to work with its beak, tearing apart its hard-won meal.

McGrew WC (1980) Gabar goshawk drowns its prey. *Ostrich* 51: 53.

93 SCAVENGING

At Assirik, over periods of weeks or even longer in the field, we craved fresh meat, which was unavailable. Tinned animal protein, usually sardines or corned beef, can satisfy for only a while. We would fantasise about burgers and sausages, a form of collective self-torture, but occasionally a solution presented itself. We could join the other scavengers in seeking fresh kills made by local carnivores, for example…

Once we heard a single lion roaring in the night, repeatedly, and someone said it must have made a kill. So far as we knew, lions in PNNK hunted only at night. In the morning we went in search of this prospect and found a partly-eaten sable antelope. This ungulate species was the third largest in the park, as big as a horse, so the lion had eaten only half of the hind quarters, leaving behind the other three-quarters of the carcass. Presumably he retreated to shady cover to digest by day, intending to come back the next night for another meal, although he then might have to compete with spotted hyenas. We went to work, flaying and butchering, and brought home kilograms of meat. We then ate meat for three meals a day, until it started to go off, so we added curry powder in increasing measures until it was too rank for us. From the beginning, we smoked strips of the meat to make biltong/jerky, which lasted longer.

Another time, we were sitting in Stella's camp, having lunch, when a bushbuck ran past, just metres in front of us. The reason for its flight quickly became clear – it was being pursued by a pack of African wild hunting dogs. After lunch, when we returned to the bush to chase chimpanzees for the rest of the day, we found the bushbuck, dead and damaged but otherwise untouched. Presumably it had eluded the dogs but later died of its injuries. What followed was a similar sequence of opportunism and feasting.

I've never been a hunter, but I am happy to be a scavenger.

94 WILD BAKING

Westerners seem to be obsessed with having daily bread, although few of us actually bake it. This fixation was true even in rural West Africa, especially in Francophone countries. Even the smallest village seemed to have a *boulangerie* where one could buy baguettes baked fresh daily. What to do in the bush?

At Assirik, we would stock up on bread on our supply trips, but these occurred only every 4-6 weeks, and especially in the rainy season, bread did not stay edible for long, as it began to mould. Of course, we cut off the mouldy bits and kept eating what remained, but eventually the bread was finished, long before the next supply trip.

Baking bread actually can be done easily in a field camp, as flour, yeast and water are really all the ingredients needed, plus the labour to mix the dough and knead it. The challenge is the oven, so we improvised. We put a few inches of water into an ordinary galvanised metal bucket. In it we stacked tin cans left over from cooking; large ones from tinned tomatoes were the best. These we oiled and filled with just the right amount of proven dough. We then covered the bucket with aluminium foil and placed it on the wood-burning campfire. After some trial-and-error, we got the amounts and timing right, but the results amounted to only a few mini-loaves. Tasty, but quickly consumed.

Then Nigel Orbell, from Stella's camp on the other side of the mountain, took pity on us and offered to build us an oven. Excitement! He came with cement and we gathered flat stones. He constructed a simple box of stone and cement, with two grill-shelves inside, and one side open as an entrance, to be shut off by a removable metal door. Inside the box's cavity we would burn wood for a half-hour, then rake out the coals. Depending on the weather, this was enough time to raise the temperature inside the oven to bake the bread, and the coals were used to cook the rest of the meal. It was wondrous.

Of course, once the baking got underway, pizza, birthday cake, cupcakes, etc. followed!

95 FLYING CHIMPANZEE

Stella Brewer's chimpanzee rehabilitation project at Mt. Assirik was joined by an Italian woman, Raffaella Savinelli, who brought with her a young home-raised male chimpanzee, Bobo. He was entirely devoted to her as his foster mother. Raff fell in love with Patrice Marty, one of the managers of the tourist hotel in the park, but the distance from the hotel to the field camp entailed many hours driving. Patrice was a pilot with access to a single-engine Cessna, so Raff asked us to help her clear an air strip on a plateau near Stella's camp at Mt. Assirik, which we did. Thus, the two love-birds could spend time together, and it emerged that Raff could wind Patrice around her little finger.

When she asked to take Bobo up in the plane, sitting on her lap, of course Patrice agreed. I went along for the ride, so we were three human adults and one infant ape in an airplane. Once we were airborne, Raff asked Patrice if Bobo could have a go at flying the plane. Initially, he was resistant, but she reasoned that if Patrice remained at the other set of controls, then Bobo would be just a co-pilot. She pointed out that once a plane is in the air, all you have to do is maintain a state of stability, based on feedback from the plane's control panel. That is, the screen that indicates the plane's movement in three planes (up-down, right-left, tilt). If you keep the dot on the screen in the central position, the plane just flies straight ahead, to put it simply.

With Bobo at one set of controls, Raff showed him what he needed to do. He was a quick learner, so Patrice eventually removed his hands from the other set of controls, and for what seemed like an eternity, but was really less than a minute, I think, Bobo flew the plane, solo. Amazing!

However, there were limits to Patrice's acquiescence. When Raff suggested that Bobo might now try to land the plane, Patrice declined, with my support!

96 WATERHOLE WATCHER

These days, camera 'trapping' (CT) is a great boon to field workers studying unhabituated populations of chimpanzees. A remote camera with a motion-detection feature that captures images of creatures that pass within its visual field yields otherwise unobtainable data about shy or wary subjects of study. Not only does CT accumulate information that leads to individual identification of the apes, it also supplies images of sympatric wildlife, such as predators, prey, and competitors. Moreover, CT can photograph nocturnally active species via infra-red, including predators on chimpanzees, such as leopard or lion, which are rarely or never seen by diurnally active primatologists. Development of this useful technology has been made possible by digital systems and improved batteries, plus declining costs of the equipment, due to popular interest in the activity.

Most sought after is imagery of the subjects in action, that is, doing something of interest, such as foraging, socialising, tool-using, grooming, etc., but even resting in the company of others yields information about social relations.

These differing goals raise issues about sampling validity, which leads to decision-making about placement of the camera. To capture images of termite fishing, an extractive foraging behaviour, one must site the camera near a termite mound, and preferably one that has yielded indirect evidence of use by the apes, such as abandoned fishing tools. What to do about grooming, which can take place anywhere? The camera trapper must usually accept that the probability of gaining useful data may be small, taking place in just a fraction of the total time that the camera stands ready. So deciding where to put the camera, within the landscape of the apes' range, is crucial.

The latter constraint led to our devising a precursor of CT at Mt. Assirik, decades before today's camera traps were imagined, much less employed. The Assirik chimpanzees may range over the largest area of any wild chimpanzee population, so just finding them was a challenge.

How to localise them? We realised after the first dry season, which lasts for seven months without rain, that drinking water was a major limiting factor for the chimpanzees, who prefer to drink daily. As surface water dried up, the options of places to drink shrank accordingly, but we noted that one waterhole, not so far from our camp, was one of the last to disappear. It was a depression in the laterite pan, so the rocky substrate lacked vegetation, making it ideal for unimpeded viewing of its users. Furthermore, for the same reason, it lacked mud, so was not of interest for mud-wallowing species, such as warthogs, which meant the water remained potable.

During our next break at the University of Stirling, we asked the technicians if they could devise a remote camera that would sample attendance at the waterhole. Ingeniously, they made a sturdy aluminium box for an inexpensive Super-8 mm cine camera that used colour film of the kind that people used in the 1970s for home movies. They installed in the box a forward-facing light meter that was sensitive to ambient illumination, connected to a switch that turned on the camera at dawn and turned it off at dusk. The camera could be set to take a single-frame shot of the waterhole at given intervals, such as 15 seconds. The device worked on standard, rechargeable batteries, and these, along with film, had to be replaced every fourth day. We set it up in a shady shrub nearby, so, for about 12 hours a day, the 'waterhole watcher' was ready to film the waterhole's visitors.

What did we find? Lots of kinds of animals came to drink, including mammals, reptiles and birds, the latter being most common. The mammals ranged from large-bodied ungulates, such as roan antelope, to small rodents, such as ground squirrels, and thankfully, they included chimpanzees. Attendance was more frequent at the beginning and end of the day, and, of course, there were other users at night, which we missed. Thus, we obtained data on chimpanzee and patas monkey sharing the same vital resource, which at the time was unimaginable, given that patas monkeys are among the inhabitants of the driest and most open African ecotypes. A far cry from the evergreen rain forests of the African tropics!

Why did we not publish our findings? The explanation is embarrassingly simple: We were too lazy. Consider that in a day, set at 15-second intervals, the camera generated about 2880 images, totalling over 20,000 in a week, with the vast majority containing nothing more than small birds. So frame-by-frame analysis by hand was tedious and time-consuming, and the rolls of film piled up and up. Somehow, we always found a reason to focus on more exciting and engrossing data, so the proper analyses never got done. In retrospect, this was reprehensible, and you may search the 40+ scientific publications that resulted from the Stirling African Primate Project and find no mention of the waterhole watcher. *Mea culpa!*

97 REVENGE OF THE VILLAGE DOG

At the end of a season of chasing wild chimpanzees at Fongoli, in Senegal, I needed to get from the field in the extreme south-east to Dakar on the west coast. The journey covers hundreds of kilometres, and time was short until my flight from Dakar in two days' time. From there, I was booked to fly back to Scotland to resume teaching. A Senegalese friend, Sadi Sall, offered to come and pick me up, saying that a friend had a car, and they were looking to get away from the city, for a break. I happily accepted their offer.

We set off from Kedougou in the morning. Not long

afterwards, we passed through a village, where Sadi's friend, who was driving, hit a dog that did not get out of the way of the car in time. This collision happened because we were going too fast, despite my attempts to get him to slow down. He was a city boy, not used to having village animals wandering in or across roads. Goats especially are a hazard! He was reluctant to stop, as the dog was clearly dead, worried that he might have to deal with an angry owner, so we pressed on.

Within half an hour, when we were deep in the bush, the car suddenly came to a stop. Inspection showed that the radiator had been seriously damaged in the collision and had run dry, so, we were stuck beside the road. A look in the car's boot revealed no tow-rope, so even if we could get a passing vehicle to stop, we had no rope to enable a tow to the next town, Tambacounda. All that we could do was try to flag someone down and hope that they would help us out. Many cars passed without pausing, and the day got hotter and hotter.

Finally, a truck stopped and offered to help, but the driver had no tow-rope either. He suggested that we could make a tow-rope by braiding together vines from the nearby forest. There were big, sturdy- looking lianas there, and so we did. This took some time, but eventually we rigged the tow and set off. This cobbled-together device lasted for about 50 metres, then snapped. So, we resumed roadside waiting and hoping.

Eventually, in the late afternoon, the driver of a vehicle with a tow-rope took pity on us and towed us into Tambacounda. There we went to the nearest roadside garage, where the head mechanic diagnosed the radiator as irreparable. He offered to scour the local scrapyards for a replacement radiator and told us to return the next morning. When we did, he had four radiators lined up as potential replacements. Road accidents on bad roads are not uncommon in rural Africa, and wrecked vehicles are routinely taken to scrapyards, where their usable parts are salvaged and re-cycled. He filled each one with water and we waited to see if any were suitable, but unfortunately, each one leaked copiously. He assured us that there were no other appropriate radiators in the town.

At this point, Sadi spied a car of the same make and model as ours parked at the back of the yard. He then asked the head mechanic if he would *rent* us the radiator from that vehicle, paying in advance. The mechanic was dumbfounded by the suggestion. He explained that the car belonged to a client who was on leave in France. He also immediately countered by asking how could he be sure that we would return the radiator, once we got to Dakar? Sadi was ready for that, saying that he could send along one of his junior mechanics to travel with us, who would never let the radiator out of his sight. This proposal persuaded the head mechanic and pleased the junior one being given a free trip to the capital city. So off we went, in a win-win-win situation. Later, in Dakar, I made my flight, and we all had a story to tell. I hope the radiator got home.

98 PYGMIES

Knowing that I worked in equatorial Africa, chasing chimpanzees, folks sometimes ask if I met pygmies. My response is that I had only one opportunity, working with Elizabeth Rogers at Belinga, in northern Gabon (see 73). There we hired local pygmies to help us find and track the apes, as they were hunters with superb knowledge of the forest.

These hunter-gatherers did not live the lives that one reads about in classic ethnographies, which verge on the idyllic. At Belinga, they had taken residence in an abandoned mining prospecting camp, which was remarkable in its own right. Decaying and becoming overgrown by the jungle, it had villas, carports, even tennis courts and a swimming pool. Amongst the buildings, the biggest was the former motor pool, which must have housed trucks, tractors, diggers, etc., but it was now just cavernous empty space. This 'cavern' the pygmies had filled with makeshift huts, retaining their family-based separate dwellings salvaged haphazardly from materials left behind.

Instead of trading with the local Bantu people, that is, forest products swapped for agricultural crops, which means bush meat protein for tuberous carbohydrate, they prevailed upon us to take them to the nearest village for this exchange. We anyway had to go periodically for our own supplies, so we tried to work out a schedule for these trips, such as every fortnight. But this failed, as inevitably, on some morning, the trackers would tell us that they were unable to work because they were out of food. We would then remonstrate, asking what had happened to the food brought back by the last trip, according to schedule? Why had they not given us advance warning that food supplies were running low?

This predicament somehow could not be explained, but they were out of manioc (cassava, a carbohydrate-rich tuber), so we had to go earlier and more often than planned. This state of affairs was in keeping with the well-known generalisation about tropical foragers, that they do not store food, and so live on a different sort of rhythm from the sedentary rest of us.

Once we got to the village, the men and women separated,

with the latter heading for the market to get provisions, while the former went in search of alcohol, so on the trip back half our passengers were inebriated or had passed out.

At one point, we enquired about getting a glimpse of their traditional life, outside the mining camp, so they agreed to take us to a hunting camp, deep in the forest. We set off on foot and eventually came to a clearing, where we found the arrangement to be just as in Colin Turnbull's classic ethnographic descriptions: a collection of simple huts made from bent-over saplings covered in shingled leaves for roofs. In their midst was a dampened campfire, beneath a rack, where chunks of meat were being smoked. It was all very ethnic, and true to form, they generously invited us to join them in a meal of the proceeds of their hunting.

As this was being palavered, I glanced down at the smoking rack and saw *movement* in the meat! How could this be, as they were just butchered portions of meat, not living, whole animals? A closer look showed the movement to come from maggots, in abundance. It seemed that near the edge of the rack, it was not hot or smoky enough to deter flies from laying eggs. I then began to worry which chunk of meat my portion would come from, and whether I would be expected to eat the maggots (perhaps as a sort of garnish?) or merely try to brush them off, inconspicuously. Luckily, as it happened, my meat came from a central piece, tough and flavourful, but lacking extras.

99 PIRATES!

Lake Tanganyika is huge, big enough to be tidal, and its hundreds of kilometres of shoreline have no real cities. Instead, most of it is villages or forest. Thus, there is potential for villains to practise piracy, as they can fade into the bush after making their raids.

At bedtime one evening, during a field season at Mahale Mountains National Park in western Tanzania, we heard a knock on the door. One of our Japanese colleagues, Michio Nakamura, was holding a black plastic bag, into which he asked us to put our valuables, such as money, passport, camera, etc. He explained that word had come up from the lakeshore that pirates were going to raid our camp that night. To keep our valuables safe, he was going to deposit them in a safe hiding place in the forest. That precaution made sense, but what about *us?* Michio explained that we researchers should sleep in the bush that night, hiding as well, so we were told to grab some bedding and follow him out of camp.

Off we went, far enough away that we were unlikely to be found. We spread a tarpaulin on the ground and settled down to try to sleep. Thoughts of army ants, snakes, spiders, leopards, etc. occupied us, but it was mosquitoes that made their presence felt. We were meant to be silent, communicating only in whispers and showing no lights, but one of our number, a nicotine addict, insisted on smoking. The pungent scent surely would have given us away, and another person's snoring also might also have done so. It was a long, uncomfortable night, and no one got a good night's sleep.

No one disturbed us, either human or other critters, so at

dawn, we trekked back to camp, feeling slightly embarrassed, especially when we met the cook humming as he made breakfast, completely as normal. He didn't say a word, just went about his business, but others later confirmed that no pirates had come. I've sometimes wondered if it was a prank played by the staff, to see how gullible we might be.

100 FLYING TO THE FIELD

Recently in the news was the account of the crash of an ill-fated Boeing 737-Max 8 flying by Ethiopian Airways from Addis Ababa to Nairobi. I flew that route on that airline in the original 737 model, back in the 1970s. When the research grant money allowed, we flew by western airlines, but when finances were tight we flew on the cheaper airlines, such as EgyptAir, Nigerian Airways, etc. These carriers were notable in that they sometimes weighed the passengers as well as their luggage, presumably because they were cutting payloads as close as possible. Back then, local airlines were flying second-hand (or more) planes that had been retired from service on bigger airlines. We used to joke about whether or not they might fall apart en route. We could not imagine then that in the future, planes would crash because their operating systems had got so complicated that pilots were overruled by computers.

Such scheduled flights to the field get you only to a major city, which is just the start of the journey to the field site. My most memorable part of the final stage was flying from Kinshasa into the interior of the Democratic Republic of the Congo to study bonobos. The vehicle was a six-seater Cessna single-engine prop plane, and the carrier was an organisation run by and for Christian missionaries. They flew on a charter basis to remote air strips in the rain forest. Before take-off, the pilot paused to pray at the end of the runway. The journey took us over what seemed to be endless miles of green carpet, occasionally containing narrow ribbons of brown. The carpet was the upper canopy of the unbroken rain forest, and the brown ribbons were watercourses.

The surprise came at the destination, when our descent revealed that we were about to land on a short gravel strip cut out of the jungle. Clearly it afforded little margin for error, and if a mishap occurred, there would be no rescue or support services. Apart from a lone windsock, there was nothing. No building, vehicle, much less a radio mast or a control tower, but land we did. Afterwards, while the plane was unloading baggage, I paced out the width of the landing strip. It was 11 metres wide, not much wider than the wingspan of the aircraft.

McGrew WC, Marchant LF, Beuerlein MM, Vrancken D, Fruth B & Hohmann G (2007) Prospects for bonobo insectivory: Lui Kotal, Democratic Republic of Congo. *International Journal of Primatology* 28: 1237-1252.

101 POACHERS

Most of my field work was done in African national parks, from Senegal to Tanzania. By definition, these are protected areas, in which hunting of wildlife is banned, but many of the parks were created in recent times and so overlay areas that earlier provided traditional resources for local people. (Fig. 10) Thus, conflict can exist between locals and conservationists, especially if the formers' prey are endangered species. All the African great apes have IUCN endangered status, so field primatologists are drawn into the fray, like it or not. The most serious cases for primate researchers are when their study species is sought by illegal hunters, such as with mountain gorillas, or when hunting techniques directed at other species present hazards for apes, such as snares set for duikers that catch chimpanzees.

Of all the places where I chased after chimpanzees, only one required field workers to be accompanied by an armed park guard. That was Toro-Semliki Wildlife Reserve, in western Uganda, close to the border with the troubled Democratic Republic of Congo (DRC). Only once while working there did we encounter poachers, a pair of unarmed men with poaching gear but no prey. The guard apprehended them at gunpoint and turned them over to law enforcement officials.

At most places, the poachers avoid the researchers and vice versa. One might find snares (to be destroyed or confiscated) or other traces of their activities, such as spent cartridge cases, or even hear gunshots. Sometimes the traces took some figuring out. Imagine finding a ring of freshly-cut leafy branches, loosely arranged in doughnut or domed shape around or over a drying-up water-hole, late in the dry season. What to make of it? A local person explained it as a device for catching colourful songbirds that came to drink, in which the poacher lurking in nearby bushes dashes out to cast a net over the waterhole. Briefly obstructed in their flight by the leafy device, the birds are entangled and caught. These birds, such as fire finches, are not for eating but for sale to dealers who send them to Europe for the pet trade.

Lui Kotale (an unprotected area) in DRC had the most serious of all the poaching problems I met, and the situation was more complicated than usual. Poachers from outside the area were after bush-meat in the same place where researchers were doing a long-term study of bonobos. The former were well-armed and shot mostly medium- and large-sized mammals, from colobus monkeys to elephants, but they did not shoot bonobos. Thus, those two stakeholders could co-exist, however uneasily. When we met poachers on the trail, sometimes armed with AK-47s, we kept the encounters to a minimum.

Problems arose when the poachers needed to replenish their food supplies, especially carbohydrates. They came to the research camp, offering to trade meat for cassava, but were politely declined. They then went to the local village, seeking the same exchange, but this raised the locals' ire, as these outsiders were decimating the locals' wildlife, setting up hunting camps in the locals' forest. Impressively, the locals mounted a punitive expedition, armed mostly with spears and machetes, but with one archaic shotgun which looked likely to be more hazardous to the shooter than the target. They came to the research camp, seeking our assistance, so some of us joined them. We found the poachers' camp, which seemed to have been abandoned hastily, perhaps because they'd got word of the irate locals on the way. The intruders had an impressive operation for the mass smoking of prey, which was necessary in order to take meat out of the forest and transport it long distances to cities for sale before it went off. Scores of dark grey, gutted carcasses of colobus were stacked like cord wood under shelters, along with various other kinds of wildlife. Colobus monkeys were said to be vulnerable, because when surrounded by hunters they headed to the tops of trees. Such a strategy normally worked against terrestrial predators, but not for humans armed with firearms, when the poachers sprayed the canopy with bullets, the monkeys fell like fruit in an orchard. Poachers can come in handy, however. In areas where the authorities can afford to mount organised anti-poaching patrols, the most successful of these are ex-poachers who have gone straight!

102 HANDEDNESS

Few basic aspects of human behaviour are naturally universal. A clue to such phenomena is their presence across all human cultures, even after extensive research seeking exceptions. One of the simplest of all is handedness, that is, preferential use of the right or left hand, for a variety of manipulatory tasks. Researchers have yet to find a single society that is predominantly left-handed. Instead, in any given human society, about 90% of the population is right-handed, while about 10% is left-handed. This stark result is notable, as its measurement is so easy, being a binary choice, either one limb or the other. On the other hand, ambidexterity is not simple, is uncommon in all human societies, and is graded, not binary. For example, baseball players commonly throw right but bat left.

Of course, culture influences the manifestation of handedness. Some human cultures suppress use of one hand, while others promote it. Historically, Western schoolchildren were trained to write right-handed, even if it took punishment to make them comply. An extensive, controlled, experimental study of mice raised in a lateralised environment showed that it was possible to induce either a left- or right-handed population. But is human handedness unique?

If handedness occurs in non-humans, we might expect it in our nearest living relations, the chimpanzee and the bonobo, giving us a clue to its evolutionary origins. Because human handedness correlates with cerebral asymmetry and apes show similar asymmetry, we might expect to find humanlike handedness in apes. Many scientific studies of chimpanzees' manual behaviour have been done, but despite the simple, either-or measure, the results are unclear. Why this problem?

Most studies of handedness in both species have used only a few measures, rather than the whole behavioural repertoire, and for the apes, most studies have been done in captivity, rather than the wild. Either constraint could produce misleading results. The commonest variable in human studies is handwriting, a behaviour that is absent in chimpanzees. Most captive apes live in environments created and used by humans, most of whom are right-handed.

In the early 1990s, Linda Marchant and I could find no study of apes done in nature using a comprehensive range of behavioural patterns. Over the next 20 years we did various ethological studies of chimpanzees in the wild, recording all their distinguishable, manual behavioural categories and some of their pedal ones as well, as controls. For months we studied whole communities of these apes at Gombe and Mahale. All individuals except for babes in arms were included. Some data were also videotaped, for cross-checking. In all, we produced 26 publications on manual laterality from 1991-2013.

In the process we encountered many methodological problems, which made the studies less simple than you might expect. For example, consider the manual task of dealing playing cards. In contract bridge, the dealer places 52 cards on the table, one by one, in four piles of 13 cards, typically in an unbroken sequence. Should that completed deal count as 52 events, or 13, or four, or only one? Suppose the dealer pauses mid-deal, puts down the deck to scratch his nose, then picks up the deck and continues dealing to the end of the deck? How many events is that? We adopted conservative criteria, counting an unbroken deal as one event, and a 'broken' one as two or more, depending on the number of breaks. Most other studies of handedness did not even mention this problem, much less try to account for it.

So what did we find? Chimpanzees *do* have a form of handedness, although we called it task preference, rather than hand preference. For some tasks, they consistently used one hand but not the other, but this occurred on an *individual* basis, not a *population* one. In both groups that we studied extensively (Gombe and Mahale), the population's overall performance by preferred hand use did not depart significantly from 50:50, left versus right. Some exceptional tasks *were* significantly lateralised. These were ones requiring more skill, such as fine manipulation done using precision hand grips, such as termite fishing (TF), which entails carefully threading a probe into a termite mound for extracting its occupants. (Fig. 3) These tasks tended to show extreme lateralisation, such as 100% by one hand or the other, but still the laterality was individually left or right, not populationally biased.

Several unexpected findings emerged, all of which were revealing. For example, for one such skilled test, another example of extractive foraging, arboreal ant fishing (AF), there was no lateralisation. This alerted us to another variable, previously neglected: in AF, the chimpanzee uses one limb to support its body-weight, hanging suspended as it fishes from the tree trunk with the other hand. Analysis showed that an AF ape switches limbs periodically, presumably to relieve fatigue in the supporting one. Overall, this results in no preference, at both individual and population level, for this activity. No previous studies had paid attention to the non-preferred hand.

In another study we looked at function in bottom-line, quantitative terms; exclusively lateralised chimpanzees (i.e. who used only one hand) were more efficient at TF than others who were incompletely lateralised. This finding linked to a longer-term aspect of chimpanzee life: frequency of TF by adult female chimpanzees compared with their life-time reproductive success. We found positive correlations, that is, those who fished more often had more surviving offspring, shorter inter-birth intervals, etc.

What if we applied similar methods to human beings, especially those living traditional lifestyles (e.g. non-literate, rural)? We applied comprehensive ethological methods to three such societies, extracting data from a cinematic archive of the Max-Planck Gesellschaft in Andechs, Germany. (56) These groups were: G/wi San (foragers from Botswana), Himba (pastoralists from Namibia), and Yanomamo (horticulturalists from Venezuela). All three showed weaker right-handedness compared with WEIRD (Western, educated, industrial, rich, developed) societies. However, in all three of them precision-gripping tool use was normally done exclusively with the right hand.

Simple handedness turned out to be more interesting than expected!

Marchant LF, McGrew WC, Eibl-Eibesfeldt I (1995) Is human handedness universal? Ethological analyses from three traditional cultures. *Ethology* 101: 239-258.

McGrew WC, Marchant LF (1999) Laterality of hand use pays off in foraging success for wild chimpanzees. *Primates* 40: 509-513.

Marchant LF, McGrew WC (2007) Ant fishing by wild chimpanzees is not lateralized. *Primates* 48: 22-26.

Mackworth-Young C, McGrew WC (2014) Elementary technology correlates with lifetime reproductive success in wild chimpanzees, but why? *Pan Africa News* 21: 12-15.

103 HONEY'S COSTS

Chimpanzees are suckers for honey. They are willing to risk the painful stings *en masse* from African 'killer' bees in order to get it, using 'smash and grab' techniques. They are not the only ones to pay costs...

One day at Gombe, two of us researchers and two field assistants were following a canny old male, Evered. The assistants followed first, then researchers, in single file, behind him through the undergrowth. Suddenly, there were shouts from up ahead of '*nyuki!*' and Evered and the assistants disappeared – here one moment, vanished the next. By the time we researchers had mentally processed the Kiswahili word for 'bee', the insects were upon us, and all we could do was to run pell-mell, retracing our steps, while we flailed and swatted and got stung. We ran downhill, pursued by the bees, but then we reached the shore of Lake Tanganyika, still beset.

What to do? No time for deliberation, so we flung off our field equipment, that is, cameras and binoculars and tape recorders, and plunged into the water, fully clothed. But the bees kept after us! We then took to diving underwater to evade them, but whenever we ran out of breath and surfaced, they were waiting for us, circling above the water, to renew their attack.

We were saved by a poor soul who had nothing to do with any of this but got caught up in events anyway. He was a fisherman who was drying his *dagaa* catch on the pebble beach. These are minnow-sized fish, caught at night and then sun-dried by day. As soon as we arrived with the bees he had sensibly retreated into his hut to avoid them. When he retreated, the baboons nearby lurking pounced to steal his fish! Thus, he faced the dilemma of staying under shelter from the bees but seeing his catch stolen, or rushing back out to chase away the baboons and risking being stung. He chose the latter, and the bees transferred their attention to him. Too bad for him, good luck for us.

104 INDIAN INTERLUDE

Field primatologists normally end up choosing among three continents to pursue their careers: Africa, Asia, or South America. These are where the wild primates are to be found. You may quibble that Europe has Barbary macaques on Gibraltar, or that some monkeys range up into Central America, but basically it's a three-way choice. Once committed, especially to long-term field studies lasting decades, it's hard to switch. So, I became an Africanist, as chimpanzees range only there, south of the Sahara, but I did have one powerful temptation to tarry.

Out of the blue, a friend and colleague at the University of Stirling, John Bancroft, asked me to join him on a trip to India. He needed a zoologist to balance up his botanical expertise in an exploratory trip to India at the behest of the UK's Overseas Development Administration. ODA was responding to a challenging request from Karnataka about advancing the conservation and preservation of the Western Ghats, the chain of mountains that runs north-south on the western side of the Indian subcontinent. It contains many endemic plants and animals, among them the rather spectacular lion-tailed macaque, an endangered species of monkey in which the males sport a mane like a male lion. Hence, my primatological invitation.

Why challenging? Because we were to be hosted by two somewhat uncomfortable bedfellows, the Bombay Natural History Society (BNHS) and the Karnataka Forestry Department (KFD). The former was India's primary proponent of wildlife protection and research, thus preservation; the latter was tasked with managing and sustainably harvesting timber, thus conservation. The two basic aims, although overlapping, are not the same, as one party cuts down the forests in which the other party's organisms must survive. John's and my task was to come up with a plan for research and training of staff of both organisations to advance the efforts of both, in cooperation.

We flew first class to Delhi (by British Airways, of course), to meet with folks at the British High Commission, which was to be our base. Once briefed, we flew on to Bombay (now Mumbai), where we acquired our companion (minder?) from the BNHS; our brief visit involved being wined and dined at what had been a colonial club in the days of the Raj. Then we flew on to Karnataka to meet officials at the KFD, who were to provide our accommodation and sustenance in the field. We exchanged business cards, as was usual then, but while ours from Stirling were made from mere paper, theirs were made from wafer-thin pieces of sandalwood. When tucked in your shirt pocket, their wonderful scent reminded you from then on of their origin. Cool!

We were housed at the high-class West End Hotel, with lovely terraces and gardens and seemingly unending supplies of Kingfisher beer. Of course, we were taken along to another ex-colonial club, although it couldn't match its counterpart in Bombay. Finally, we headed to the field, to be shown the state of the Ghats and to be told what needed to be done, using ODA's money. The forests were verdant and impressive, although travel was sometimes slow along mountain roads. At the end of each day, our entourage would pull up at one of KFD's guesthouses, which were scattered around the

Ghats, for visitors. These were well-appointed and yielded surprisingly tasty and bounteous meals of local food, given that we were far in the bush. Each morning we would be wakened by the raucous sounds of crowing jungle fowl, sounding like domestic chickens, which is not surprising, as the former were the ancestors to the latter. There were a few drawbacks, such as ever-present leeches to be detached.

John's trip was made worthwhile (so he said) by being shown and walking along one of Harry Champion's original forest transects, cut over a century before, but still maintained by the KFD (76). My high point was seeing lion-tails up close and personal, working their way through the canopy, while their sympatric cousins, pig-tailed macaques, foraged on the ground below them. Passing like ships in the night. Of the cultural and natural sites that we were shown along the way, the one that stood out was a tree laden with the larvae of fireflies, winking in their hundreds (thousands?) in unison.

Back in Delhi, with lots of notes and papers, we debriefed at the High Commission before flying home. For reasons unknown, the required BA flight back to Heathrow was unavailable, so we were forced to fly Singapore Airlines. Too bad!

Back in Stirling, we dutifully wrote up the required report with our carefully balanced recommendations. Eventually, a version of it was approved and funded, and John went back to India to help implement it, but my interlude in India was done.

105 PRIMATE ARCHAEOLOGY

This sub-discipline of archaeology ultimately refers to how past primates behaved, and by definition this means knowing about actions unavailable for first-hand observation. If past behaviour is inaccessible, then the next best thing is the products of behaviour in the form of enduring objects or traces, that is, *artefacts*. In the archaeology of humans, especially after the emergence of symbolism, artefacts, whether paintings or inscriptions on cave walls, imprints on clay tablets, or hieroglyphs incised in stone, may be informative. The older archaeological record before symbolism is not so conveniently direct, and its utility or meaning must be inferred carefully.

Such challenges resemble those facing the primatologist seeking to study wary and elusive living primates, who avoid contact. They too leave behind artefacts of their acts, to be found, collected and interpreted, usually in context with other traces, such as tracks, hair, faeces, etc. While the archaeologist of extinct humans has no chance to meet his subjects alive, the primatologist studying extant subjects can at least aspire to habituate them and so acquire behavioural data. Having both behaviour and artefacts makes primate archaeology doubly productive. (75)

For example, wild Japanese macaques engage in 'stone-handling', a puzzling habitual behaviour that takes many forms and results in piles of stones left around the landscape. At Arashiyama, outside Kyoto, the monkeys can readily be seen in action daily. But would these artefacts be recognisable outside their context of observed use? We collected handled stones and a similar (control) sample of stones eroding out of a hillside and gave a mixed array of these to Cambridge students who knew nothing of the behaviour. They could distinguish spontaneously the two types, thus satisfying a basic requirement of archaeology, that is, validity.

When we moved from Gombe's totally habituated chimpanzees to Assirik's totally unhabituated counterparts, we were forced to adopt some techniques from archaeology, from surface surveys to careful preservation and curation of remnants. Assirik chimpanzees' termite-fishing tools, collected by my student, Norman McBeath, are now deposited in the Scottish National Museum, Edinburgh. (Fig. 26) But primatologists are not archaeologists, and looking back now, I see that are our etho-archaeology barely scratched the surface, so to speak. For example, excavation, site-mapping, assemblages, palimpsests, etc. were absent from our early work. Nor are archaeologists trained in primatology, which meant other kinds of gaps in data, in the early days.

It took a new generation of researchers to develop primate archaeology. The leading proponent in the field is Susana Carvalho, who has rare equivalent credentials in both disciplines. She is as adept with a Total Station as with a video camera and works at well-established palaeo-anthropological sites such as Koobi Fora (Kenya) and at long-term chimpanzee sites such as Bossou (Guinea). (Fig. 24) Her team at Oxford pushes the boundaries: Alejandra Pascual-Garrido focuses on the 'archaeology of the perishable', that is, organic artefacts that degrade and disappear, but before that still can be traced to source.

What about digging? Excavation is somehow thought to be essential to archaeology, whether of Egyptian tombs or layers of sediment in Upper Palaeolithic caves. The key is in the term 'lithic' (stone), which endures for eons. The leader in that aspect of modern primate archaeology is Michael Haslam, who has excavated and dated stone tools used hundreds of years ago by capuchin monkeys in Brazil and long-tailed macaques in Thailand.

The birth of modern, integrated primate archaeology can be traced to a seminal conference held in Cambridge in 2008, organised by postgraduate students and post-doctoral researchers. It brought together the two disciplines, linking both theory and practice. Such is the advance of science via successive generations.

Carvalho S, Matsuzawa T & McGrew WC (2013) From pounding to knapping: How living apes can help us model hominin lithics. In: Sanz C, Call J & Boesch C (eds), *Tool Use in Animals: Cognition and Ecology*. Cambridge University Press, pp 225-241.

Haslam M *et al.* (2017) Primate archaeology evolves. *Nature Ecology and Evolution* 1: 1431-1437.

McGrew WC, Matsumoto T, Nakamura M, Phillips CA & Stewart FA (2014) Experimental primate archaeology: Detecting stone handling by Japanese macaques (*Macaca fuscata*). *Lithic Technology* 39: 113-121.

Pascual-Garrido A & Almeida-Warren K (2021) Archaeology of the perishable: ecological constraints and cultural variants in chimpanzee termite fishing. *Current Anthropology* doi:10.1086/713766.

106 BOA CONSTRICTOR

Most field primatologists end up focusing on primates in Africa, Asia or South America. In that sense, having chosen chimpanzees, I was an Africanist for 40 years. I was woefully ignorant of the primates of the other two continents, so when a late opportunity arose, I jumped at it. Eduardo Ottoni and Tiago Falotico invited Agumi Inaba and me to visit their study site in Serra da Capivara National Park, in north-central Brazil. There they studied bearded capuchin monkeys, an intelligent and challenging species, known especially for their varied tool use (see **107**).

One day while following the monkeys, we were alerted by their alarm calls. They had moved from the ground to the trees, and by triangulation, we could see that they were focusing their anti-predator responses on the forest floor below. From their vocalisations, it was likely to be a snake, we were told. So, we approached the focal spot to investigate. Four of us stood around an area of about one square metre, scrutinising the leaf litter, but no matter how we searched, we could see no sign of a predator. Seconds, then minutes went by, and we saw nothing. Perhaps it was a false alarm?

Then, out of the brown leaves, a flicking black tongue appeared. There, amazingly camouflaged, was a 1.5 metre-long boa constrictor, an ambush predator, patiently lying stock still. It had been an impressive feat of detection by the monkeys, but for me it was a long-awaited opportunity, given my herpetological roots. (7) Like many other snake-charmed persons, I had dreamt of catching such a serpent, and here was my chance. I used one hand to grasp its neck and the other its tail. The latter coiled powerfully around my arm, reminding me that it killed prey by throttling it, not by venom. Photos were taken, and my day was made! (Fig. 27)

107 MONKEY TECHNOLOGY

Over my primatological career, I devoted more time to chimpanzees' tool use and their material culture than to all other topics combined. I extolled in books and articles these apes' superiority in elementary technology above all other living non-human species. (Fig. 12) Perhaps you can imagine my chagrin when these claims were called into question by Burmese long-tailed macaques and bearded capuchin monkeys (see **106, 108**).

My forced retreat came on two fronts. First, I began to read of the behaviour of the capuchins in the dry Caatinga habitat of Serra da Capivara National Park, Brazil, from the research team of Eduardo Ottoni and colleagues. Any doubts were dismissed when they invited me to visit these monkeys in 2015, hosted by his student, Tiago Falotico. Especially notable was that the monkeys were talented in lithic technology, that is, the use of stone tools, the key element in the archaeologist record, from which inferences on the evolutionary origins of human technology are based. My previously favoured chimpanzees do little with stone tools, apart from using them to bash open nuts. These New World monkeys not only *use* hammer-stones to break open plant foods, dig up roots and subterranean spiders, but they also *make* tools by hammering and pulverizing the quartz stones in conglomerate rock, as in some cases the freed stones are then used as tools. They also make and use organic tools, such as modified sticks to produce probes to dislodge both vertebrate (e.g. lizard) and invertebrate (e.g. bees) prey from otherwise inaccessible crevices in rocks or trees. Such an extensive tool-kit for such varied purposes puts chimpanzees in the shade!

Similarly, I began to see compelling accounts of the behaviour of these Old World monkeys on offshore islands in Thailand, especially from the pioneering research of Michael Gumert. Later my concerns were confirmed by a visit to these islands, to see first-hand the monkeys in action, hosted by their main advocate.

Michael showed me the macaques of Laemson National Park, on the island of Piak Nam Yai, as viewed from a drifting boat offshore. They were akin to beach-combers, focusing their extractive foraging in the inter-tidal zone, which at low tide reveals a wealth of opportunities for feasting. Found there are molluscs (e.g. oyster, clam, snail) and crustaceans (e.g. crab), and more than 40 species are processed and consumed by the enterprising monkeys. All prey have shells or carapaces of calcium carbonate or chitin that need to be overcome by percussion, and remarkably, the monkeys have a tool-kit for these tasks. To process oysters takes a pointed tool ('axe-hammer') to peck away at them on the rocky substrate; to break into gastropods, they need a boulder or outcrop as anvil and a heavier stone ('pounding hammer'). They carry their tools from place to place, and the shoreline resounds with the sounds of banging stones, as the troop processes its seafood *en masse*.

My first attempt at salvaging the reputation of my apes was to suggest that seaside chimpanzees might do the same if they foraged on oceanic shores, as at least one population, in the Nimba Mountains, *does* use percussive technology to process freshwater crabs. I invoked the apes as the candidate champions of the terrestrial sphere, but the same macaques studied by Gumert and Co. also move inland to crack nuts, such as sea almonds, with anvil and hammer-stone. Like chimpanzees who bash hard-shelled fruits against large roots or embedded stones, the macaques do the same with coconuts. Similarly, the capuchins outshone chimpanzees by being tool-makers as well as users, on both the lithic and non-lithic fronts. No wild chimpanzee has ever been seen to make a stone tool. All three of these living primate species have archaeological records based on excavations of stone tools dating hundreds or even thousands of years old.

My retreat from chimpanzee technical superiority is now complete, having co-published with its advocates a synthetic book chapter about the triumvirate of bearded capuchin, Burmese long-tailed macaque, and chimpanzee (in alphabetical order!). Science marches on.

Gumert MD & Malaivijitnond S (2012) Marine prey processed with stone tools by Burmese long-tailed macaques (*Macaca fascicularis aurea*) in intertidal habitats. *American Journal of Physical Anthropology* 149: 447-457.

Mannu M & Ottoni EB (2009) The enhanced tool-kit of two groups of wild bearded capuchin monkeys in the Caatinga: Tool-making, associate use, and secondary tools. *American Journal of Physical Anthropology* 71: 242-251.

McGrew WC, Falotico T, Gumert MD & Ottoni EB (2019) A simian view of the Oldowan: Reconstructing the evolutionary origins of human technology. In: Overmann L & Coolidge F (eds), *Squeezing Minds from Stones*, Oxford, Oxford University Press, pp. 13-41.

108 IMPOSSIBLE BIPEDALITY

Occasionally the most rewarding results in research come by chance, that is, by the researcher being in the right place at the right time to see something which has not yet been scientifically described (see **86**). Sometimes it can be a one-off, coincidental occurrence, worth publishing as an anecdotal note, in order to alert other scientists to keep an eye out for it. Other times, it is a common occurrence that has not been reported, despite many years of observation. Here is a case of the latter.

During a short visit to Serra da Capivara National Park, in Brazil, we watched capuchin monkeys at a provisioning site. This procedure, of supplying abundant food regularly at a certain place caters to tourists with their cameras. Here, the food items were dried kernels of maize, which the monkeys collected by the handful to take away to consume alone in peace. Typically they gathered up enough to fill two hands, then changed their locomotion from quadrupedal to bipedal, walking upright on their legs with arms together in front of them, holding the food. Such situational carriage of particulate food items for a short journey by bipedality is not uncommon in primates.

These monkeys did much more. Having horizontally covered the ground to a nearby tree, they continued their bipedality into the vertical (third) dimension. That is, with hands occupied by the food, they used only their legs to climb the tree trunk. Imagine scaling a flagpole with only your bare feet! Of course, monkeys, unlike humans, have prehensile feet as well as hands. They can grip with all four limbs. Capuchin monkeys also have prehensile tails, but they were not used here. They speedily and efficiently ascended metres into the canopy, with only their soles and toes touching the tree trunk.

On the first day out, we exclaimed to our hosts about this remarkable behaviour, which they had seen so often that it had not 'registered'. To them, it was mundane. Biomechanically, it was almost unimaginable; the stress put on the spine alone was unprecedented. So, from the second day, we made systematic observations and videotaped the behaviour. We were determined to publish this finding, especially when an extensive survey of the scientific literature revealed no previous report of it. There have been many studies of capuchin locomotion done in captivity, but always on two-dimensional, horizontal substrates, such as treadmills.

So we added a bit of knowledge to the advance of primatology. Do we deserve any credit? Not really, as the phenomenon was a serendipitous gift from the monkeys.

Falótico T, Inaba A, McGrew WC & Ottoni EB (2016) Vertical bipedal locomotion in wild bearded capuchin monkeys (*Sapajus libidinosus*). *Primates* 57: 533-540.

109 BEYOND CHIMPANZEES

Considering my fixation on chimpanzees, some folks think I have studied no other species of primates. This is understandable, given that 75% of my empirical primatological publications have been on *Pan troglodytes*. If you add non-empirical papers, that rises to 85%. Actually, I've collected and published data on 17 other non-human primate species, in journal articles done in collaboration with others, mainly students. This total is but a small fraction of the living primate species, and it includes few prosimian primates (potto and bushbaby), of which I am embarrassingly ignorant. But there is some variety...

The next most common species for me is not an ape, was studied in captivity, and never seen be me in the wild: cotton-top tamarin. However, not many have seen it *in situ*, as its range is restricted to a part of northern Colombia. A vignette (53) is devoted to this research, so no more need be said about those nine papers here. Next comes baboons, as studied in West Africa (Senegal) as Guinea baboon and in East Africa (Tanzania) as olive baboon.

What about the other apes? Pretty paltry, I admit. Not a single study of lesser apes, that is, gibbons (Hylobatidae). Only five articles on bonobo (see **100**, **101**), four on gorilla, and a measly two on orangutan. The rest account for just one or two papers: green monkey (**91**), patas monkey (**91**), Tana river red colobus monkey, Hanuman langur, stumptail macaque, Japanese macaque (**105**), pig-tailed macaque, bearded capuchin monkey (**107**, **108**), common marmoset (**52**).

Perhaps I was just a 'one-trick pony' after all.

Anderson JR & McGrew WC (1984) Guinea baboons (*Papio papio*) at a sleeping site. *American Journal of Primatology* 6:1-14.

110 THREE ACES

Some people are just the best at what they choose to do. I was lucky enough to work with three such people in the field, chasing after chimpanzees. I cannot imagine how it would have been without them.

Caroline Tutin and I were not meant to work together at Gombe; she was supposed to study fringe-eared oryx in Kenya and I green monkeys in Barbados. Instead, we teamed up to study wild chimpanzees in Tanzania, in Gombe's heyday. For her PhD, she focused on sexual behaviour, following reproductively-cycling females over hill and dale. The apex of this task was to follow one of her subjects who disappeared 'on safari' with a chosen male, often to the edge of the community's range, seeking privacy. Some of these consortships lasted many days, necessitating an exhausting, unbroken string of all-day follows, with days up to 15 hrs long, for if the solitary pair were 'lost', they were almost impossible to find again.

Next, she was one of the three founding researchers on the Stirling African Primate Project at Mt Assirik, Senegal, which was the first study of savanna-dwelling chimpanzees in a hot, dry and open habitat. Finally, she and Michel Fernandez went on to initiate a long-term field study of great apes in Gabon, an ecological comparison of sympatric chimpanzee and gorilla at the equatorial rain forest site of Lope. They set standards for research methods that still apply today. She and I co-authored 28 articles together from 1972 to 2014. (Fig. 5)

Anthony Collins (also known as Anton, Ant, Tony, etc.) and I started at Gombe at the same time, in October, 1972. His PhD research was on olive baboons, while my post-doctoral study was of chimpanzees, but we overlapped daily. Youngsters of the two species played together often, which is a PhD topic that would have been superb but was never done. Gombe was lively then, with up to 20 researchers in residence, many of them keen undergraduates from Stanford University, thanks to David Hamburg. A later project, in the early 1980s, at the Japanese research site in the Mahale Mountains, further down the eastern lakeshore of Lake Tanganyika, cemented our bond in the field. Times were hard then in Tanzania, and we two were often the only ex-pats working there with Tanzanian counterparts. The markets were often bare of even basic commodities such as rice, and at times we had to cook with linseed oil, as it was all that was available in Kigoma. We undertook the first ecological study of Tanzanian chimpanzees' major form of tool use, termite fishing, which entailed cutting kilometres of transects from lakeshore to the mountains. (**76**) Ant took the lead, having spent weeks in the Natural History Museum (London), learning the taxonomy of those insects. He and I co-authored 5 articles together from 1985 to 1989. (Fig. 15)

Linda Marchant had done a PhD on laterality of hand function (handedness) in captive chimpanzees but had never done field work. Her first taste of it, at Gombe, converted her to the field, and she never looked back. There, we focused on wild chimpanzee handedness, in a comprehensive study of spontaneous behaviour in their daily lives of ranging and foraging. Later, we replicated and extended this topic in a field season at Mahale (see **102**). Other field projects on chimpanzees followed, at Semliki in Uganda and Assirik in Senegal; we did one foray into the Democratic Republic of the Congo, to the field site of Lui Kotale, for a study of bonobos. Besides ethological observations of behaviour, she also video-taped chimpanzees in action. These hard-won recordings were more than illustrative, for example, analysis of one set yielded forms of manual grips not recorded before in the species, and one won a top award for documentary filming in physical anthropology. She and I published 44 articles together from 1991 to 2015. (Fig. 14)

INDEX

Numbers refer to vignettes, not to pages.
P = preface, *F* = photographs

blue duiker 74

Blue Ridge Parkway (North Carolina) 39

boa constrictor 106

Bobo (chimpanzee) 89, 95, *F*

Boesch, Christophe 50

Bombay (Mumbai) 104

Bombay Natural History Society 104

bonobo 73, 100-102, 109

Bossou (Guinea) 72, 73, 86, 105

Boston Red Sox 50

botany 5, 76, 104

bot fly, 81

Bourbon Street (New Orleans) 13

Bovril 24

Bowes, Alison 42

Boxall, Evelyn *P*

boy scouts 4, 29

Bradley, Bill 8

Brent, Linda 59

Brewer, Stella 89, 93-95, *F*

Bridge of Allan (Scotland) 25, 80

Brown Bear (chimpanzee) 89

Bruno 89

Buachaille (Glencoe) 29

Buchenwald 22

Budongo (Uganda) 72, 73

Building Bridges between Anthropology, Medicine and Human Ethology 68

Bulindi (Uganda) 72

Bunengwa, Moshi 33

Burg Wartenstein (Austria) 48, 49

Burn, The (Scotland) 51, 54

bushbaby 73, 74, 75

bushbuck 74, 83

butchery 65, 73 109

Byrne, Richard *F*

C

caatinga (Brazil) 107

Cabo San Lucas (Mexico) 48, 60, 68

California, University of, Berkeley *P*, 55, 57, 67

Callitrichidae 52

Cambridge 35, 37, 79

Cambridge, University of 8, 22, 41, 64, 66, 67, 69, 105

- Dept. of Biological Anthropology, 64

- Leverhulme Centre for Human Evolutionary Studies, 69

Cambridge University Press 60, 64

camera trap (see waterhole watcher)

Cameron Arena (North Carolina) 50

Campbell, Robin 84

Canadian Valley Conference (Oklahoma) 8

Canavan, Dennis 27

capuchin monkey 105-109

Caribbean Primate Research Center (Puerto Rico) 71

Carmina Burana 56

Carpathian Mountains 16

Carpenter, Charles ('Doc') 5, 7, 9, 12, 42, 43

Carpenter, Mary Chapin 20

Carter, Janis 3

Carvalho, Susana 105, *F*

Cascais (Portugal) 48

Cassidy, Eva 20

Castle Hill (Cambridge) 35

Cayo Santiago (Puerto Rico) 71

cemetery 35

Champion, Harry 104

channel catfish 10

Charles, Ray 20

Charlton, Bobby 21

Checkpoint Charlie (Berlin) 26

Chicago Cubs 50

children 42, 43

Child Psychology Series 68

BV - #0074 - 071221 - C16 - 229/152/16 - PB - 9781861515827 - Gloss Lamination